Lean Innovation

Understanding What's *Next* in Today's Economy

Lean Innovation

Understanding What's *Next* in Today's Economy

BARRY L. CROSS

CRC Press
Taylor & Francis Group
Boca Raton   London   New York

CRC Press is an imprint of the
Taylor & Francis Group, an **informa** business

CRC Press
Taylor & Francis Group
6000 Broken Sound Parkway NW, Suite 300
Boca Raton, FL 33487-2742

Printed in the United States of America on acid-free paper
Version Date: 20120822

International Standard Book Number: 978-1-4665-1525-3 (Hardback)

Library of Congress Cataloging-in-Publication Data

Cross, Barry L.
    Lean innovation : understanding what's in today's economy / Barry L. Cross.
       p. cm.
    Includes bibliographical references and index.
    ISBN 978-1-4665-1525-3
    1. Technological innovations. I. Title.

HD45.C6888 2013
658.4'063--dc23   2012030321

Visit the Taylor & Francis Web site at
http://www.taylorandfrancis.com

and the CRC Press Web site at
http://www.crcpress.com

For Brad Cross and Robert Good,
brother and best friend.

I miss both of you every day.

Contents

Acknowledgments

I want to start by thanking everyone associated with bringing this project to fruition. I really had no idea what I was doing when I started out with it early in 2011, but here we are. So, to my excellent readers David Green and Cheryl (Cross) Green, Don Warren, Steve and Brenda Mercer, Katrina Cross—thank you for your advice, input, and feedback and especially your time in helping me shape this book. The perspectives and thoughts you provided were invaluable.

To the publishing team at CRC Press/Taylor and Francis—you were a dream to work with: fast, efficient, and very patient with the newbie. Thanks especially to Lara Zoble for her faith in my proposal and how quickly we got things going, and Joselyn Banks-Kyle and Jay Margolis for navigating me through the publication process. I hope we can do it again!

Thank you to those who took the time to talk to me about their innovation or their challenges with innovation. I could not have done it without you.

A special thank you again to Don Warren. I have known Don since 1990, when he brought me into a young and enthusiastic company called Autosystems, a place he built from the ground up into a very successful $200 million company. Don was a mentor and a very significant part of my development and success over the years and remains a good friend today.

At Autosystems, there were a number of key people who made that such a great place to work. Thanks to Jason Bonin (a close friend), John McDougall, Hank Jonkman, Deb Page, Robin Mills, Dave Venton, Kevin Mackey, Jeff Potter, Glenn McQuaid, Peter Newman, and all the others. Good times … .

Another mentor and friend as I migrated from industry to academics was John Gordon, professor emeritus and a member of the Faculty Hall of Fame at Queen's University School of Business. John was one of my professors when I did the MBA at Queen's and had me back a number of times as a guest speaker before helping me understand more about what it takes to be a good professor and making the introductions for me at Queen's.

Thank you to Dean David Saunders and Associate Dean Brent Gallupe for their confidence in signing me on back in 2006.

Thank you to my colleague Kathryn Brohman. The two of us have built a significant "practice" around project management and execution in the school that continues to grow and resonate with students and industry. Some of those concepts are discussed in this book.

Thank you to Peter Kissick, a colleague at Queen's, for his wise counsel with this project.

The folks at Queen's Executive Development and our marketing people have been very good to me as well. Thanks to Tom Anger, Barbara Dickson, Amber Wallace, and Glenn Cavanaugh, and their dedicated teams for helping me get it done.

My focus on innovation was initiated by a request from Julie Einarson, who asked me to look at "something different" on innovation back in 2007. Thank you, Julie; this has grown into something bigger than I think either of us would have thought at the time.

At the Garden Restaurant in Belleville, Ontario, a Chinese food buffet, my fortune cookie said, "People will come to hear you speak." That was right!

And last and mostly, thanks to my family—

To my parents, Wayne and Avrel, who followed their own path. Thanks for everything, but especially for keeping me too busy as a kid to really get into trouble.

To my children, Regan and Declan—my inspiration. Keep doing it your way. I am so proud of both of you.

To my wife, Katrina, for 20+ years of unconditional love and support. Who would have thunk?

Introduction

This book is based on material I have developed over a period of five years and was initially intended for use in executive education and speaking engagements. The first couple of years I was at it, the material itself was pretty raw, but as time progressed, it was fleshed out into its current form. In the fall of 2010, I was speaking at Deloitte's annual partner's event in Toronto, part of a series of speakers lined up for the two-day program. At the morning breakfast, I was introduced to some of the other speakers, and I was asked more than once by a fellow speaker if I had read his or her book. I quickly realized that having a book to support and reinforce the subject matter needed to be on my to-do list. I joked about this as I opened my session that morning. As I left the proceedings later in the day, I bumped into Mark Robinson, a partner with Deloitte, who pointed out that with the framework and material that I had gone through with his team that morning, I had the substance of a book in my hands already. I just had to write it.

Simple, but not easy.

My objective with this book is to help people think a bit differently about innovation, help them see things and recognize opportunities that may not be initially apparent. Lofty goals perhaps, but my approach to innovation is really very simple, and thinking differently is at the root of it. The concept of innovation feels out of reach in many cases, so I use stories and anecdotes from a number of industries to connect the concepts to the realities faced by the readers. Innovations are evaluated in their raw form as ideas, in a more refined state when they become a project, and finally when they are in the hands of a customer.

One of the challenges we face is getting over the hump from talking about innovation to doing something about it and making it a priority for the organization. Within the book, I talk about some of the road-blocks to innovation and how to use enablers like Lean to facilitate and focus our approach to driving what I call *Next* in our business. *Next* is the place where new services are satisfying tomorrow's customers. It is the place where creativity in our ranks is more important than responding to an e-mail and where the organization is not afraid to make an existing product redundant in favor of a new opportunity.

Many of you have been exposed to or have applied Lean concepts in your firm. For those who have not, Lean is about a focus on value in all areas of the business, and value is really determined by our customers.

What do they want, and what matters less to them? Applied effectively, Lean reduces and eliminates tasks, processes, products, and services that fail to create value for our customers. If you are not sure about a particular task or procedure that you currently use, ask yourself, "Would the customer pay for that?" If the answer is "no," can you eliminate it?

My perspective comes from the several companies I worked for before becoming an "academic" and the dozens of companies I have worked with since leaving direct employment in industry. The stories people tell, with a smile or a wince, led to deeper research in the press or direct contact with the companies discussed here. Some are what I would call best in class (at least for now), while others are here because their struggles highlight opportunities for us in our firm. The problems faced by most firms I have worked with or researched are very similar and reinforce the incredible challenges faced by very capable leaders in keeping a company at the forefront of its industry. Even more difficult is getting an underperforming entity there in the first place.

Before joining Queen's University in 2006, I spent 20 years in various industries—plastics, automotive, and electronics. I was able to spend time with suppliers, customers, and partner organizations in Canada, the United States, Mexico, South America, China, and parts of Europe. I led project teams, sales organizations, and manufacturing groups. I met a lot of terrific people from different backgrounds, most of whom were very motivated to make things better and drive change in their organizations.

A big part of why I wrote the book is related to these companies. Very few of them had significant resources in research and development yet, of necessity, still needed to innovate. My approach is to bridge the perception that heavy investment in research and development is necessary to shape the future of our company. More important is a culture of curiosity and challenging the status quo, of never being satisfied with satisfying only today's customers without thinking about tomorrow's, and a healthy paranoia about the challenges faced by the organization. Innovation needs to be on our agendas, and we can control our own destiny.

When I started talking to managers and executives about innovation, the challenge of sufficient resources was prevalent very early. "We don't have the people" was a common refrain. "Hmm," I thought. I had been through some true resource issues in several businesses that were growing or financially constrained. Through tools like value-chain analysis, Lean, and 6 Sigma, the Toyota Production System, we made it work (although it was not always pretty). The organization learned and improved. My belief is that most of us, through Lean, have the resources we need to innovate.

I read a lot of material on innovation, change, execution, and the larger category of *Next* for our organizations. There is some great work out there on this that I would heartily recommend. Check out *Wal-Smart* by Bill Marquard, *The Disney Way* by Bill Capodagli and Lynn Jackson, or anything by Scott Berkun on innovation or projects (humorous and insightful). *Blue Ocean Strategy* by Kim and Mauborgne presents an interesting perspective on value. There are a couple of books on major failures and how to avoid them: *Billion Dollar Lessons* by Paul Carroll and Chunka Mui or *What Were They*

Thinking? by Jeff Pfeffer. You will see references to this material in the Notes section at the ends of the chapters. In some cases I build on their idea, while in others I turn it around, tackling the concept from a different angle. I have done my best to properly attribute my sources throughout the book; my apologies for anyone I may have missed. That does not make their thoughts wrong and mine right; these books made me think, as I hope mine will with you. You will not agree with everything you read here, but I hope it gets you moving along a path beneficial to you or your firm.

The plan of the book evolves like this: Chapter 1 discusses the need for innovation and why we are talking about it in the first place. Chapter 2 is the facilitator in my innovation model and discusses Lean as an enabler. Lean is there to free up the resources we need to drive innovation and one of several tools we apply to get the organization thinking differently.

Chapter 3 introduces my innovation model, discussing and defining the key concepts of an innovation culture and how a firm can generate ideas, refining those ideas and then launching the projects that result from an idea. Chapters 4 through 7 address each of those concepts in detail.

Chapter 8 circles back to what I consider the most fundamental concept in driving innovation: organizational culture. The methods and tactics discussed through the previous chapters really do not work without the leadership team walking the walk and helping shape the organization into one that embodies higher levels of creativity.

At the end of each chapter, there is one or more short stories. These are real-life examples intended to connect the dots between some of the theory and its application. Some of the stories are what I call "cool ideas," while others may represent an innovation challenge or a poor execution of an idea. All are there to provide context and, in some cases, a bit of a history lesson.

My writing style is similar to the way I speak in classrooms or with leadership teams. It is conversational and anecdotal and really represents the way I think. You will note that the grammar and style at times may lack sophistication, but this is what feels natural to me. I am a simple guy. I try to insert some humor here and there, which

I hope you appreciate (fair warning: my wife, Katrina, tells me often how others do not find me as funny as I do).

Read the footnotes and have fun with Appendix 1. The endnotes are really there to provide more information should you seek to dig deeper or to reference the source where appropriate.

Enjoy the book and have fun with your path to *Next*, that place your organization will exist with a focus on innovation.

About the Author

 Barry Cross joined Queen's University in Kingston, Ontario in 2006 after spending 20 years in various leadership positions with several companies. While in industry, Mr. Cross led many key strategic initiatives, including significant development projects in Asia, Brazil, Mexico, and Europe.

Mr. Cross now teaches at Queen's School of Business in Operations Management, Service Management, and Project Management. At the executive level, he speaks regularly on innovation, execution, and project management. He has an MBA from Queen's University and a bachelor of science degree from the University of Waterloo in Waterloo, Ontario. Mr. Cross lives with his family in southeastern Ontario.

Section

1

Preparing the Organization for Innovation

1

The Need for Innovation

Cutting the deficit by gutting our investments in innovation and edu-
cation is like lightening an overloaded airplane by removing its engine.
It may make you feel like you're flying high at first, but it won't take
long before you feel the impact.[1]

Barack Obama

All problems can lead to opportunities—you have heard that before
(often offered as, "look at the bright side," which could seem irritat-
ing at the time). So, instead of starting with the challenges faced by
most firms today, I am going to start with a story that represents the
real upside for us in today's environment.

Let us go back to spring 2008. The problem at the time was the oil
market: Oil prices were climbing quickly, crashing through artificial
ceilings like the $100-per-barrel threshold. Analysts, economists, and
the general public were getting concerned. As oil crested at $120 per
barrel (all figures U.S. dollars), the chair of OPEC (Organization of
Petroleum Exporting Countries) was in the press on several occa-
sions, emphasizing that current prices for oil had nothing to do with
market fundamentals. Inventory was strong, and in his own words,
"There is no reason for the current pricing of oil" in the marketplace,
and that OPEC would do everything it could to restore oil prices to
their appropriate levels.[2] Indeed, OPEC increased supply, and that,
combined with other economic factors, brought oil back to relatively
reasonable levels.

Let us think about that for a minute. Here is an organization whose members basically scrape oil off the surface of the desert for a cost of about $10 per barrel, and they are worried that the price is too high. Why is that? On reflection, we understand OPEC's larger concern in this, and that is our innate capability as a society to innovate, develop, and exploit alternatives to oil. OPEC understands that at some point, we will get fed up enough with the high price of gas, fuel oil for our homes, and derivative products (polycarbonate and other engineered plastic resins all saw pricing go through the roof during that period as well) that we will do something about it. Driving habits will change; people will carpool, take public transit, or make fewer, shorter trips. We will look at vehicles with better gas mileage. We will see an increase in the use of alternative energy sources for our homes, offices, and plants. Engineers and research-and-development (R&D) labs will be tasked with better solutions for hybrid, electric, and perhaps hydrogen or natural gas vehicles, and we will get serious about it. This would result in a world that buys less OPEC oil.

The unknown factor here for OPEC? It does not know where the tipping point is. At what price does society look at and pursue alternatives and mean it? Is it $130 or $150 per barrel? Maybe the number is higher, but we do not know how high, and neither does OPEC. It does know that it is doing quite well when oil is in the range of $80 to $100 (and in fact, lower levels favor OPEC as a supplier, as Western investment in oil supply can be a challenge at those prices,* as the cost per barrel to develop supply is significant). As soon as that tipping point is reached, OPEC's market is threatened, and the members price themselves out of existence, so they try to maintain some level of perceived reasonableness in pricing. With over 80% of global oil reserves and 45% of daily production,[3] we can appreciate how this is a major area of focus for OPEC.

Where does that leave us? The moral of the story is that we are naturally creative, curious, and innovative. Many of us do not realize it,

---

* From conversations with Canadian oil executives, the loose threshold is around $75 per barrel. When oil prices are above that, investment in oil-producing assets (wells, refineries, oil sands) generally makes sense. When markets are at or below $75 per barrel, companies need to be much more selective in where and how they invest.

or believe it, but it is there. Think of an infant's wide-eyed discovery of his or her fingers ("I wonder how those taste. Only one way to find out!"), a toddler playing for hours with Tupperware and a wooden spoon from your cupboard, or that precocious four-year-old who keeps asking, "Why?" We are all hardwired for curiosity from birth, but as we grow, our education and employment systems tend to get us focusing on efficiency, process, and delivery rather than creativity and innovation. "This is the way I want it done. This is the due date." Customers are calling, e-mail is received (we talk more about e-mail elsewhere). We get very good at hitting deadlines and managing hectic schedules and do not take the time to be inspired. Worse yet, as we get better at executing, more tasks get piled on, or we get promoted to drive the same level of performance in a larger group.

You are creative—OPEC believes it, and they are worried about it. With that in mind, though, why didn't we do anything about it back in 2008? Oil prices climbed above the $140-per-barrel mark. Independent economists such as Wall Street's Robert Brusca stated that "Society can't sustain itself at current energy prices."[4] Oil billionaire T. Boone Pickens invested $60 million of his own money into looking at alternatives such as natural gas and wind energy.[5] Other than some short-term changes in our driving habits, and the odd celebrity selling a Hummer for a Prius, nothing really changed. The price of oil receded, and consumers' concerns subsided; OPEC relaxed.

We will circle back to this story in the last chapter, but recognize for now that society, like most of our companies, is subject to Newton's first law of motion (also known as the law of inertia). We tend to stay the course, whatever that course is.

The next question is: Can an organization stay the same and survive?

Okay, that was a soft, easy pitch right over the plate, and you nailed it. I speak on innovation on a regular basis, and executives and managers respond overwhelmingly "No" or "Not for long" when I pose that question. The barbarians are at the gate. Competition is too strong. Investors are impatient. Top employees will leave if we are not challenging them. We know all the reasons. Innovation and "managing change," however, are not easy targets for most of our firms.

Let us consider three firms:

- Company A understands that it needs to change and be innovative on an ongoing basis to be competitive. This is a continuing process for the company, and part of its culture, having evolved through a number of versions of itself over a company history of 75 years. It has fond memories of where it came from but appreciates that the customers of that company are long gone, as will their current customers be if they stand still.
- Company B appreciates the need for innovation, but the economy and industry factors are not right at this time. It does not believe it has the resources to innovate and is focusing on managing today's business. It is too busy serving today's customers; it is not inclined to worry about tomorrow's customers until tomorrow gets here.
- Company C would also like to be more innovative but does not possess the skill set necessary to drive "what's next" in its business. It recognizes this, however, and that concern is what keeps leadership awake most at night.

It sounds like Company A is doing just fine. It recognizes the need for innovation and works hard at it. We respect Company B's position, and in some cases would say that it is right—sometimes we just have to worry about getting the job done today and lay low for a while until things get better. Company C seems like the obvious candidate for innovation guidance or input.

In reality, all three firms would benefit from a fresh perspective on innovation, and even leadership at Company A would agree. They recognize that to be successful, they need to look outside the firm, benchmark their capabilities, seek best (and worst) practices, and most important, acknowledge the challenges they face in developing new or improved products and services on a continuing basis.

I work with an international electronics company on a regular basis. These are good people in an innovative company already, but like Company A, the company keeps at it with training, education, speakers, consultants, and benchmarking. These tools are all embedded in the makeup and drive of the firm.

Company B represents a significant opportunity, and likely an example of many of the readers of this book. A challenge we all face from time to time is the overwhelming pressures in our daily work environment, where it seems we cannot get anything done. There is too much going on, too much complexity, too many meetings or phone calls to focus on where we go next.

Another company I spoke to a few times works like Company B. It had a massive business transformation plan launching that year and wanted me to facilitate its executive training in support of the plan, but it could never find time in the calendar to make the training (or even the conference calls they were asking for) fit the schedule. Meetings and business travel were getting in the way of its core initiative.

What if I was to say to Company B's chief executive officer (CEO), "You have enough people to get everything done. You have enough resources to drive the next phase of your business. Your challenge is that the firm is wasting resources (people, space, time, money) doing things that don't matter." Company B's CEO would likely smile and hire another consultant. Company B, and organizations like it, *can* focus on tomorrow's customers while supporting today's.

This is a very real situation, and the genuine opportunity that started this chapter; our evolution through this book, starting in Chapter 2, will be to show firms that they have adequate resources but are not effectively using those resources. Once this is illustrated, I show how to free up the resources and then get the firm driving toward an effective innovation culture. In fact, it is difficult economic times like we have witnessed in the last several years that present opportunities for proactive and agile organizations to create and strengthen their innovative advantage.

Let us take a step back first, however. Is innovation really necessary for a firm to survive? This is not the same as "Can your firm stay the same and survive?" For fun, let us look at the exception that proves the rule: the Toronto Maple Leafs hockey club. Year after year, the team sells out its stadium and has attendance statistics near the top of the National Hockey League. Yet, year after year, it also struggles to make the playoffs, and if it does make the "second season," it bows out in the early rounds. In a bizarre marketing move in 2007, it celebrated its 40th anniversary of winning their last Stanley Cup (or put another way: "Hey, it's been 40 years since we've won the league championship! Let's have a parade!"). It is the richest franchise in hockey, able to afford to do whatever it wants yet really does not do anything different year after year.[*]

For most of us, it is different. We have to grow, to refresh, to adapt, to change, or our customers go away, investors leave, or competitors take our business. If we are not innovating, where will our growth come from?

A key tactic firms can employ is growth by acquisition, something we do not spend much time on in this book. Acquisition works well for many firms; Cisco, for example, has made a science out of identifying and buying companies that can add value to its product mix and talent pool. Google also does well here. The majority of firms, however, struggle with this strategy. In a study by Bain Consulting of 250 executives with mergers and acquisition responsibility in their companies, the historical data showed that the majority of takeovers or acquisitions failed to add value for the acquiring firm.[6] In a lot of cases, the acquisition actually destroyed value. Look at the 1999 purchase of Chrysler by Daimler AG. Daimler paid $36 billion for Chrysler, citing potential synergies, purchasing and logistics savings of $3 billion per year in the combined firm, possible design platform sharing, and so on. We know what happened in the end: In a complicated deal, in 2007 Daimler paid $650 million to Cerberus Capital Management to take Chrysler off its hands.[7] The Chrysler acquisition effectively destroyed almost $40 billion in value for Daimler. Innovation is far cheaper. Suppose Daimler had spent, say, $5 billion of that money on R&D and innovation instead? What would be in your driveway right now?

Consider the timing of an innovation strategy for a moment. If we look back at Company B again, let us say it puts off any consideration of innovation for three years, time enough to get its arms around the

---

[*] For what it is worth, I am a Montreal Canadiens fan, so picking on the Leafs comes naturally to me.

current operational issues it has stated are a priority. If those in leadership are successful with that objective, they effectively deal with the challenges facing today's organization or possibly today's customer. Those customers are happy. Employees take a breath. Maybe there are bonuses and high fives around the table in the management conference room. Now, they agree, we can focus on the company's future and set up the leadership retreat to map out *Next.*

There are several issues with this strategy for Company B and firms like it. The first is timing. Innovation is not something we can turn on and off like a switch, as addressed in further discussion. More significantly, the efforts of innovation will take months or years to get through the development and launch process in just about any firm. So, after three years of focus on current operations, it will be, say, another two years before the new products or services make it through the pipeline. That is a long time without any new offerings or improvement to existing offerings. Customers who were reasonably satisfied with the improvement to service delivery after the operations focus will see the lack of change as a stale offering. Competitors of Company B have been busy innovating over that same three-year period and have launched upgrades and new services.

Customer loyalty, especially in services, is only as good as a lack of a better alternative. Switching is easy.

The second, though subtler, issue is one of company culture. An operations focus for Company B is going to be all encompassing in this scenario. Executive leadership, management, and all front- and back-office employees will hear the mandate and drive the business toward improving operations. I have been through this, and it is not fun. Efficiency, customer metrics, uptime, delivery time, and help line satisfaction indices will all be on the firm's balanced score card, getting daily and weekly visibility with leadership. Employee town hall meetings will begin and end with management reporting on how Company B is doing in its three-year plan to strengthen its business. That focus on efficiency will embody the culture of the company.

Most of us are wired one way or another. At our best, we are either very efficient or very creative. Most of us understand this about ourselves. You know people who will tell you that they are not creative or creative people who cannot seem to manage a schedule or a bank account. Further in the book, we talk about how to get creativity out of all of your staff, but for now acknowledge that people bend in one direction or the other. The good folks at Company B have been driven toward efficiency *hard* for three years, and now that they have achieved their operational goals, management will tell them that it is time to innovate. "We need your ideas!" Adapting an organizational culture toward creativity and innovation is like turning an ocean liner; this is a slow, determined process. There are no switches to throw here. Company B should have kept some focus on innovation through its operations initiative to preserve some spirit of creativity and at least help it hit the ground running when it was able to commit more resources to innovation.

The reality is that "day-to-day" issues do not go away, so a dual mind-set is required. We need to manage today's customers while we think about tomorrow's.

Think of the employees at Company B who were of a creative spirit three years ago. Being forced to suppress that ability and initiative will lead those people to leave the company. New employees hired over the same period would have been screened for their ability to drive the operations side of the business. Without maintaining some focus on innovation through that three-year period will result in Company B losing the ability to be creative. The innovators are gone.

The final consideration on the need to innovate requires some level of reflection on the future of our business. Most of us do this on an annual basis, or perhaps more often, as part of our strategic planning process. I tend to take a short- and a long-term view on planning. Specific plans, tactics, and projects should go out no more than three years for most industries. That is the short term. Get specific, commit the right resources, be vigilant with follow-up, and execute well. In the long term, however, let us be realistic. We really do not know what the industry is going to look like 10 years from now. We do not know what our customers are going to want, how what they want will be delivered, or who are customers even are.* Technology, tastes, habits, capabilities, and resources are evolving faster and faster. How many of us knew 10 years ago that we would *need* a portable device that held over 1,000 songs? Apple convinced us that we did, and now most of us have at least one iPod. Kodak, whose engineers invented digital photography, is not even in the digital camera game now because leadership did not perceive the business would evolve in that direction (more on this in Chapter 7).

Key traits for leadership in any firm are humility and an open mind. We need to be humble enough that we do not assume customers will want our product or service forever, and that we do not take their loyalty for granted. With that comes an understanding of the necessity to make our own products or services redundant. That is a fundamental characteristic in innovative companies. We also need to be open-minded enough to see different paths in the evolution of our business and be willing to invest and uncover where those paths can take us.

I work with a couple of large government-owned corporations. Both are monopolies in their markets. In both cases, leadership of these organizations struggled to see that its monopoly was not based on any real advantage provided to consumers. In fact, in other markets, far better models for their services exist—more efficient or more price competitive models. Worse, their consumers are aware of better opportunities in other markets, so dissatisfaction exists. Until recently, leadership for these two firms has not understood this threat. Now, leadership realizes the companies are just a policy shift away from a major customer and competitor swing in their market. Frontline employees, however, push back against any structural changes that may lead to faster, leaner, or more effective customer service. This makes for a challenging existence.

---

* We exclude NASA and like organizations, which *are* thinking specifics out 10–20 years. Mars anyone? As well, mining and mineral companies I have worked with look out at least 10 years on their production assets, as it can take that long to get permits for a new site in place and start production from the mine. Similar timetables exist for energy production—hydro and nuclear plants.

Let us focus now on firms that do have a growth mandate, are not hunkering down and looking only at current operations. As part of that planning exercise we discussed a moment ago, these firms inevitably develop a set of measurable corporate objectives. They may look something like this:

30% of sales from products or services that did not exist four
  years ago
10% growth in earnings per share
25% return on capital
20% return on equity

If those goals sound aggressive, think of 3M, which looks for 40% of sales to come from products launched in the last five years. This kind of goal setting sends a clear message to employees and the marketplace that 3M is an organization that embraces change.

The core message in this chapter is one of necessity and need. Without an ingrained culture and commitment in our organization toward discovering, filtering, refining, and then launching new ideas, we will not survive. By all means, there are times when any firm will need to put a full-court press on their customer service or manufacturing operations. After all, that is what brings customers in our doors today. While we manage those operations, however, at least some part of the company needs to be focusing on *Next*.

Successful companies here act and behave differently. They look for opportunities. They listen to customers. They ask suppliers for ideas and have a means to track those ideas as they evolve. They have a network of advisors who help fill the gaps between ideas and execution and refine the ideas from the 1.0 version to something the market wants. They are just as concerned with what their customers will look like in five years as what customers want now.

Does this sound like your firm?

In the next chapter, we combine a couple of seemingly disparate topics: Lean and innovation. We look at Lean principles in the interest of starting to shift company culture but more importantly as a method of freeing up resources within the firm to support and drive innovation activities.

INNOVATION AT CVS PHARMACY: REIMAGINING THE PRESCRIPTION FULFILLMENT PROCESS

Remember the images from TV or movies of people hanging out at the drugstore back in the 1950s and 1960s? There was a soda fountain, spinning stools and a long countertop, apple pie, sometimes a jukebox in the corner. The drugstore was the Starbucks of that era, the place people went when they were not working or at home. Those images, or the memories of such places by your parents or grandparents, seemed very pleasant.

How many of us could say the same about our current experiences at today's version of a drugstore. There are literally thousands of locations across North America now. They sell everything from prescriptions to cosmetics to groceries to computers. Convenience is now a key part of the strategy, and generally, these stores all do a decent job in most areas of their service.

The exception has been the pharmacy, and by design, it is the most challenging part of the operation to run. Safety is a prime concern, especially with reactions to drugs or complications resulting from a patient taking more than one drug at a time. The cost of prescriptions continues to escalate. And then, there is the customer.

One of the fundamental considerations through this book is the perspective of the customer, and contrary to our image of earlier drugstores, people do not go to the pharmacy because it is an enjoyable experience. Think about the frame of mind of customers entering a pharmacy. They are not happy, smiling, and looking forward to a positive experience. They are sick, or their loved ones—children, spouses, parents—are sick. They would like to get in and get out as quickly and efficiently as possible.

In most cases, however, an efficient prescription process seems like an unrealistic expectation for our customers. We make them wait in line; the process of filling a script takes longer than it should, especially for prepackaged medication. There are also surprises at pickup; the medication may not be ready, or the customer is told that his or her insurance will not cover a $250 prescription. Combine the two elements—stressed customers and an unreliable prescription process—and it is no wonder customers get upset.

CVS Pharmacy realized it had a problem in 2001 and in 2002 launched its Pharmacy Service Initiative (PSI) as part of the "Customer Easy" campaign. How bad the problem is was not obvious; the pharmacy business drew several million new customers to CVS the previous year, outpacing defecting customers by about 3%.[8] The economy was growing at the time, CVS was adding new stores, and the business was growing. In an environment where no pharmacy chain really had it figured out (they were *all* marginal), did management really need to do anything?

What if another pharmacy got the prescription process figured out before CVS? Customers already defected to other pharmacies all the time, and switching was easy. In a service business, customer loyalty is only in place as long as there is not someone better next door. CVS Chairman Tom Ryan certainly was not happy with mediocrity and launched the PSI.

The pharmacy process is shown in Figure 1.1. Customers would drop off the script for fulfillment and return after work or running some errands or simply wait in the store. While the customer was away from the counter, the problems surfaced. There was no inventory for that particular drug in this location. No refill was permitted by the patient's doctor on that script. The customer's insurance would not cover the medication. The drug would react with something else the customer was taking at the time. In most cases, the customer would not find out there were problems until he or she returned to pick up the prescription: Queue the fireworks.

The PSI team, including CVS leadership and pharmacy representatives, along with support from Boston Consulting Group, reviewed tons of data, watched the process in stores over an extended period

Figure 1.1 The prescription fulfillment process.

of time, and identified over 60 problems with the current script fulfillment process.

Ultimately, the solution was simple. CVS was letting its customers get away too quickly. Imagine a restaurant that takes a customer order and then the chef tries to figure out food allergies or how the customer wants a steak cooked from the kitchen. Worse, the server took the order, but the restaurant is out of steak.

CVS went to work and unintentionally borrowed concepts from the restaurant business. What questions do we need to ask a customer at the table to succeed in the kitchen? The PSI team modified the process to support gathering all the relevant data while the customer was still at the drop-off counter: "Do we have your contact information, including cell phone?" "What other medication are you taking?" "Let's check our inventory for that drug." "Let's verify insurance before you leave as well."

Yes, CVS was asking its customers to hang around for an extra minute or two at the counter, but the benefit for that time was huge. There were no longer any surprises at pickup. Any medical or insurance issues that were realized at drop-off could be dealt with, often at that time. If something else arose during the filling process, the customer could be called on his or her cell phone to work it out. No inventory? "We can have it brought over from our sister store for pick up, or you can stop over there yourself. We will send the script over on your behalf." If the customer's insurance would not cover the drug, a less-expensive generic version can be suggested, or the customer could take the prescription anyway and resolve the payment issues with his or her employer or insurance provider.

Through all this, CVS was giving the customer back *control*, something lacking in the earlier process. Did it work? Reports from CVS leadership indicated that defections decreased dramatically. Revenues went up over $700 million in the first year after the changes to the process. The other, unexpected benefit was that human resource (HR) costs went down.[9] Happier customers meant less stress and a better work environment for employees, so turnover decreased. Everyone won.

Lean Innovation is often that simple, but it starts with a mandate for change from leadership. *Next* is attainable, and we are going to do it now. It is a reapplication of resources, the elimination of waste, and the introduction of elements borrowed from other industries. In this case, prior to the changes from the PSI, there was significant waste in the system. The process could be stopped several times during the production of a prescription package for a customer while staff tried to deal with missing information or other related issues. A simple, smooth process drives customer enthusiasm.

We revisit the CVS story elsewhere in this book, but first we need to look further at Lean.

NOTES

1. http://www.brainyquote.com.
2. Thorpe, J., "Saudis said set to boost oil output," *National Post*, June 16, 2008.
3. For more on inventories and statistics, see http://www.opec.org and http://www.cia.gov and the CIA's *World Fact Book*.
4. Watson, T., "Fuel prices over a barrel," *Canadian Business*, June 11, 2008.
5. Alsever, J., "Pickens natural gas idea picking up steam," October 21, 2008, http://www.msnbc.com.
6. Harding, D., and Rovit, S., *Mastering the Merger: 4 Critical Decisions That Make or Break the Deal*, Harvard Business School Press, Cambridge, MA, 2004.
7. Isadore, C., "Daimler pays to dump Chrysler," May 14, 2007, http://www.cnnmoney.com.
8. McAfee, A.F., *Pharmacy Improvement at CVS*, Harvard Business School Press, Cambridge, MA, October 20, 2006.
9. Eder, R., "New initiatives lay foundation for strong results," *Drug Store News*, August 18, 2003.

2

What's Lean Got to Do with It?

Have a place for everything and keep the things somewhere else.

That is not advice, it is merely custom.

Mark Twain

Congratulations on proceeding to Chapter 2. You have acknowledged that innovation is necessary, crucial to the future of your firm.* The easy part is over, however. *Next* is a difficult place to get to, fraught with doubt, failure, questions, expense, and conflicting priorities along the way. How do we know this is the right path for us? How do we know what customers will want (especially tomorrow's customers)? These are key concerns, indeed.

The ambiguity associated with *Next* is one of the most significant roadblocks we face. Here are some typical questions and related discussion:

- How soon will it launch? What testing is required? How about regulatory approval? That always takes longer than we anticipated (even when we take Hofstadter's law† into

---

* Or, you are stuck in an airport between flights and someone abandoned this book on the seat next to you. Regardless, happy reading!

† Hofstadter's law states (humorously) that the task always takes longer than anticipated, even when taking into account Hofstadter's law. (Source: Falkenstein, E., http://www.overcomingbias.com)

account). For example, the company's track record for execution has not been great. The longer it takes, the less likely we will hit the estimates.

- What are the potential revenue and profit estimates? This is so dependent on timing, customer interest and enthusiasm, and perhaps most important, our track record for innovation in the past. Think of Apple versus, oh, almost anyone. Another big factor is how quickly we can evolve an innovation past the current version to where it will actually make money (more on this in Chapter 5).
- How will the competition react, and what is the competition working on right now? This is marketing strategy 101, right?
- Will our customers like the new product or service? How quickly will they adopt it? Often, we will make a mistake in this area by asking too many questions of customers and putting significant weight on their responses. In reality, customers do not appreciate *Next* until they get there. Clayton Christensen's work on disruptive innovation showed us that.[1]
- Where will we get the people to pursue this opportunity?

Aha! There we are. The fifth point is the justification we are looking for in not doing anything. With the uncertainty associated with the first four points, why would I proceed? With all the pressures on the firm to succeed today, *Now* is where we need to focus, not *Next*. That was Company B's position in the last chapter.

Here is an example that embodies this sentiment: In 2007, the U.S. Department of Energy launched a contest called the *L Prize*.[2] Their pursuit? The next-generation lightbulb (big idea symbol please!). The objectives were a bulb that

- Lasts 25,000 hours
- Consumes less than 10 watts of power
- Produces as much light as a 60-watt incandescent bulb
- Takes fewer than four engineers to install (okay, that last part was my addition)

The prize? The successful party would receive $10 million. Four years later, in August 2011, Philips was crowned the winner. Philips' EnduraLED "bulb" uses LEDs* rather than tungsten filament, and to date, samples have been burning successfully for over 9,000 hours. Philips admits that while priced at $40 per bulb, household penetration may not be significant, especially since it is still overcoming some uniform illumination issues. It sees the bulb eventually dropping to $25 per unit, which should have a positive impact on customer uptake, I guess.

But, based on prior experience, the government is not done at an investment of $10 million on this one. When compact fluorescent bulbs and LED Christmas lights came out, the feds offered up rebates and incentives to stimulate demand for people to buy the products. The lower net price to consumers increased production volumes, and manufacturers were able to drive real prices down.

Projects like this involve significant research and development (R&D), resulting (it is hoped) in what we will call *New Knowledge*. *New Knowledge* is fundamental and necessary for us as a society but obviously involves substantial heavy lifting, work many of our firms are not equipped to do. The $10 million prize in the Philips' example may not cover its expense going into the project, although their eventual market is anticipated to be much larger. The firms we picture with that kind of muscle are the 3Ms, GEs, Motorolas, Samsungs, or Boeings of the world. There are years of development, millions of dollars, and hundreds or thousands of people involved in developing *New Knowledge*, and like the L Prize, we have to commercialize it. Again, this is essential to society, but that kind of effort is beyond most of us. We are grateful that companies like that exist, but most of us need an easier way.

The other challenge with the R&D side of things is that investment in *New Knowledge* is often one of the first areas of the company's budget that gets cut or frozen in tough times. The payoff is further out, and the impact on today's customer will be minimal. A company

---

* Light-emitting diodes. Circuits have been developed in the last 10 years that will produce a "white" light, facilitating their use in ambient lighting, automotive lighting, and stadium lighting at much lower levels of power consumption and operating cost.

needs to hit this quarter's earnings, so it slashes R&D—not pretty, but far too common.

Somewhere between *Now* and *New Knowledge* is the place called *Next*, and that is where we want to go. *Next* defines progress for the organization and embodies the implementation of ideas and creativity to the delight of our customers. It is the firm's goal and destination.

So, the title of this chapter is "What's Lean* Got to Do with It?"

There was a survey done by management gurus Gary Hamel and Gary Getz; C-level executives and senior managers of 500 large firms were polled and asked about the largest challenges they faced in implementing strategy (strategies, to be very clear, that include significant growth and innovation targets). The overwhelming response? There was a lack of resources and an abundance of short-term thinking.[3] They knew what they wanted to do, but believed they did not have the people, space, time, or money to do it. I ask a similar question of executives in our leadership programs: What is your biggest problem, related to the execution of your innovation strategy or its related projects?[†] We are talking about innovation, creativity, or execution. My straw poll usually ends up reinforcing the Fortune 500 one. It is about resources—people, space, time, and money—that is what Lean has to do with it.

Unfortunately, Lean has a dark side. Tell your team on Monday that you are launching a Lean initiative, and some of them will update their resume. People perceive Lean as being about cost cuts, head count reductions, and other painful processes by which we try to do more with less. That is the bad rap that Lean is unfortunately labeled with most often in the workplace today, but that is not what it is about.

For me, and the firms I have worked with, Lean is the enabler. Lean is about value. Value is the single-minded focus on what the customer wants. This is a tough concept to grasp, especially in light

---

[*] For clarity purposes, I capitalize Lean when it applies to the core context of the book. When I refer to the verb (e.g., leaning in the doorway), I use lowercase.

[†] Credit to a friend and former colleague of mine, John McDougall. When I entered his office, he would say, "Give me your biggest problem."

of my previous remarks that the customer may not know what he or she wants. So, let us circle around it for a minute.

Lean has its roots in places like the Toyota Production System* and Eli Goldratt's theory of constraints.† As such, we often think of it in a production context, but it applies very much to services as well, as will be discussed further. Focus on smooth flow through your process, eliminate the bottlenecks and excess inventory, and you will deliver on time and keep customers happy—sounds simple.

Lean has also been linked in recent years with Six Sigma, the problem-solving and error-reducing tool worked hard in industry by companies like GE and Motorola. Apply Six Sigma, and you will reduce mistakes, downtime, or out-of-spec parts, and free up capacity and dollars in your process. This part is less simple, but very effective in firms that take it seriously.

The real opportunity for us in the context of innovation comes from a dialogue on why firms pursue Lean. The causal factors driving Lean initiatives are such things as challenging business environments and competition, a perception that costs are too high (usually overhead costs), and finally business complexity. Of the three, the most sustainable justification for the pursuit of Lean in this context is complexity.

Complexity? Let us connect the dots. At Queen's School of Business, we did a survey in 2010 with roughly 130 leaders and managers who were part of the executive MBA programs at Queen's University. Over 70% of the respondents believed their businesses had too much complexity. Looking further, over half of them agreed that their customers did not understand or appreciate all of their available products or services. So, we say we have too much complexity, and our customers do not understand everything we are trying to provide them. I can hear some of you saying, "Hmm ... "

Some examples are warranted. Think about the menu board at your local Starbucks. Most of us order one of four types of beverages: coffee, tea, latté, or cappuccino. Over the years, however, the menu

---

* See, for example, *The Toyota Way* by Jeff Liker (McGraw-Hill, 2003) and further references in Appendix 2.
† See *The Goal* by Eliyahu Goldratt (North River Press, 1992, book or movie version).

at Starbucks has grown increasingly complex, to the point where the poor baristas were struggling to make everything accurately and efficiently, especially when most of us customize. Starbucks has recently started to simplify their core offerings, but the entire chain of stores is still shut down periodically to support employee training.[4]

It is also a challenge for customers. Reflect back to the first time you entered a Starbucks, probably with a friend or colleague who had been through the process. You looked at the menu board, and the line of people around you, and felt anxious, the anxiety increasing as you approached the counter. "What if I get it wrong?" "How do you pronounce that?" "That thing is $4—what if I don't like it?" Anxiety? Bad decision risk? Absolutely. Starbucks has done a great job creating a market around that "affordable indulgence" category, but the complexity still creates issues. Most customers order derivations of those four main beverages, yet the menu board lists a dozen others, and baristas need to be able to make everything well.

On the product side, consider General Motors. Until President Obama told them a few years ago that they were not getting any bailout money until they simplified their organization, the folks in charge at GM were convinced they needed a dozen different brands: Chevrolet, GMC, Pontiac, Buick, Oldsmobile, Cadillac, Saturn, Saab, Izusu, Hummer, Holden in Australia, and Opel in Europe. Those same executives were also convinced that some of their customers would only drive a particular brand, say a Pontiac. Maybe they were right. I have not met that guy, but perhaps he is out there. Think about it, though: In maintaining those dozen brands, you have distinct engineering and marketing departments, separate administration, separate dealer networks, and often separate production facilities. A Chevrolet pickup truck and a GMC are basically the same vehicle, yet each can take millions of dollars in unique tooling to build, hundreds of engineers to launch it, and advertising money to support it, and the dealers who sell the trucks are probably located across the street from each other. How much sooner would we have seen the Chevrolet Volt electric vehicle in dealer showrooms if GM had diverted some of its investment in brand proliferation to new core technologies?

Examples like this are everywhere. Canada Post purchased Purolator Courier in 1993, yet already owned and operated Priority Courier, an overnight logistics provider in the category created a couple decades ago by FedEx. It would seem appropriate to shut down one of those operations and consolidate systems and resources, but the two organizations are currently subject to a regulatory agreement that states they must retain their autonomy and run Purolator and Priority right next to each other*—double the aircraft, double the trucks, double the people, and so on. Does this make sense? The role of regulation in innovation needs to be focused on safety, preventing a group from repeating past mistakes, and driving growth in appropriate sectors of the economy. It should never force an organization to maintain an unreasonable operating structure in the interest of protecting jobs.

My new favorite example is Maple Leaf Foods, which thankfully saw the light early in 2011. Before launching a Lean initiative, Maple Leaf had 78 different recipes for wieners.[5] Yes, that was 78. Every time its production line changed over between wiener varieties, the line was down for as long as 90 minutes. By the way, they also had 50 different sizes of wiener-like products.† How many sizes do you really need? I am thinking three: the big ones that you load with mustard and sauerkraut for outside the sports stadium, the "regular" size for kids' birthday parties, and I kind of like the little cocktail weenies on occasion that you poke with a toothpick because they are just fun. Fifty? Come on. Credit the leadership at Maple Leaf for moving this situation in the right direction. While most of us would not face the anxiety of bad decision risk when it comes to our wiener purchases, too many product choices can dilute your brand and in this case was causing some awkward production scenarios with recipe changeovers and downtime.

Your organization has some of this going on as well. Most do. These excess products or services that overlap each other are a result of a lot of things. Think acquisitions and mergers, where *they* had a product

---

* From a conversation with a Canada Post Corporation executive.
† Also referred to as franks, hot dogs, jumbo dogs, and foot longs.

like one of *ours*, and we left both running when we bought *them*. We launch a new credit card for customers of our bank, but leave all the existing ones status quo. Some long-time product offerings exist only because sales executives have successfully argued for years that they have customers who will leave if that offering is discontinued.

Information technology is also partly to blame. Storage and processing capacities have grown exponentially, which means *we never throw anything away*. Rare among us is the individual who sticks with the 2-GB USB memory key and deletes files when it gets close to full. Most of us upgrade to the 16-GB device, which we can now purchase for $10, and hang on to all of our files forever.[*]

We come by this naturally enough. It is our farmer heritage; out of necessity, we kept everything in case we needed it again since a trip to Home Depot was not an option. My uncles in Saskatchewan still farm. I remember visiting as a kid, and a tractor had broken down. For farmers, uptime of their equipment is critical during seeding and harvest, when they often put in 18-hour days on 2,000-plus acre properties to get the work done before the weather changes. An out-of-service tractor could pose a significant issue. So, my uncle headed out to the "shed,"[†] found a suitable replacement part, and got the tractor going again within a couple hours. Most of us came from a farming background at some point or another, and old habits die hard.

All of our organizations have too much complexity: product or service proliferation, legacy products from past periods, slow and inefficient internal operations, even our meeting and communication culture within the organization. When was the last time you were part of a really good meeting? Most companies struggle with people arriving late, e-mail distractions, redundant updates, or missing information. That is another form of waste, and we can do better.

Connect this to the three companies in Chapter 1. Company B wants to be more innovative but does not have the resources. Now, think about the examples in this chapter: Do any of these situations sound familiar to you? If we could deal with that complexity, would

---

[*] My friend Steve Mercer refers to this phenomenon as the insecurity associated with insufficient knowledge.

[†] The sheds in Saskatchewan are about the size of a barn for most of us.

you be able to free up resources to focus on more important tasks? My premise is that *most firms have enough people, space, time, and money to do the things that need to be done, but they are wasting those resources on tasks, functions, and processes that do not add value.*

The challenge here is identifying the waste. We cannot send our people forth and say, "Conquer the waste and complexity!" We will get blank stares and calls for our replacement. So, we need to provide context and frame the situation for our employees.

My purpose here is to provide a few simple little exercises that can help an organization understand that maybe there are some activities going on that we do not realize in our day-to-day operations: activities that bog us down; processes that frustrate suppliers or create anxiety for customers; excess products in our portfolio that are still around because we have not had the courage to drop them. Part of what we are after is a paradigm shift, recognition that we can start to do things differently. Good leaders recognize opportunities, avoid catastrophes, and break paradigms. Awareness is the first step in shifting our organization toward an innovation culture.

While we use Lean in this book as an enabler innovation, we will move past it as a core topic after this chapter. There are already whole books and papers on Lean that map the process better than I can (see Appendix 2 for a decent starting point for your reading list).

THREE STEPS TO A LEAN CULTURE SHIFT

Step 1: Watch and See

Bookmark this page and open your Internet browser to YouTube. In the YouTube search bar, type in "awareness test." Dozens of videos show up on the list, but near the top will be a group of people in white and black uniforms playing basketball. This one is my favorite example, and was created by Transport for London as part of its cyclist awareness program.* With a very sophisticated British accent, the narrator says, "This is an awareness test. How many passes does the team in white make?"

---

* See, for example, www.tfl.gov.uk/corporate/media/newscentre/metro/10456.apx, November 20, 2008. TFL is a YouTube hit.

How did it go? Did you say 13 passes? Yes? But, did you see the moonwalking bear? Most of us do not, at least not the first time through the video. There are lots of these types of clips out there: moonwalking bears, gorillas doing kung fu. When we are told by the narrator what to focus on, however, we miss what seems obvious the second time through the video. Connect this back to your own organization. How many times in the past have you noticed something with a fresh pair of eyes that the people inside the process have not noticed despite their familiarity with the routine of the activity? People totally outside the operation are even better at this: customers, suppliers, executives and board members, consultants. Fresh perspectives and fresh eyes can be a huge asset in helping us "see."

The conclusion is that things are happening around us, and we do not see them, complex things that consume resources or behavior that frustrates customers or other stakeholders. In November 2008, for example, the top executives of Ford (Alan Mulally), Chrysler (Robert Nardelli), and General Motors (Richard Wagoner) all traveled from Detroit, Michigan, to Washington, D.C., to meet with high-level government officials and request billions of dollars in aid to help their floundering companies. The problem was one of optics: All three execs traveled separately in private company jets. "There is a delicious irony in seeing private luxury jets flying into Washington, D.C., and people coming off of them with tin cups in their hand, saying that they're going to be trimming down and streamlining their businesses," House Representative Gary Ackerman told the chief executive officers (CEOs) at a hearing of the House Financial Services Committee.[6] Until they were called on it by the representatives of the committee, the CEOs saw nothing at all wrong with their behavior, all the while asking for money and forcing the rest of their organizations to look for ways to trim operations.

Step 2: Think and Learn

In step 2, we engage the brain a bit further. For example, tell the team you want to take a fresh look at the English alphabet. The world is flat: People are studying, traveling, and doing business all around the globe now, and everyone is dealing in English. But, the English language is peculiar in that we have some odd spelling and grammatical rules as well as some redundant letters. The task before us is to simplify the English alphabet. We want to take it from its present state of 26 letters to something a little more streamlined. We want to be able to make the same sounds, but we need to do it with fewer letters. Yes, some adjustments to spelling will be made, but that is a sacrifice you are prepared to make.*

At the start, people on your team will look at you with a strange expression but will eventually smile and proceed (easier than arguing with a crazy person). When someone offers up a letter, you write it down and ask how to make the "_" sound. For example, take out the letter *C*, and the hard *C* sound will be made with *K* and the soft *C* sound with *S*. Within a few minutes, your whiteboard will look like this:

Deleted Letter	Replaced with
C	K, S
F	Ph
Q	Kw
J	Soft G
Y	I or E
Z	S

More courageous groups will suggest an *X* can leave in favor of Eks (in x-ray) and *Z* (in xylophone). If you have a Russian in the room, that person will have no use for *V* (in favor of *W*). Then, put a goofy phrase up on the board:

> The kwik brown phoks gumped over the phense.
> (The quick brown fox jumped over the fence.)

Now, they are *thinking*. Take a line from your company vision statement and use the same Lean alphabet.

> We are kustomer phokused!

In some cases, it will be the first time the people in the room have read the vision statement and actually thought about it. The advantage of this approach is we are circling around waste and complexity

---

* To paraphrase Lord Farquaad in Shrek.

without focusing on any of our company processes yet. Therefore, people do not feel threatened and yet are starting to understand that we are not seeing everything we need to see. A few people who have gone through this exercise with me push back a bit: Doesn't this actually increase complexity in the English language? Won't learning a new alphabet create anxiety and work for people that counteract the simplicity I am searching for? My answer is that, sure, this would be a learning process for everyone. Could we do it? Absolutely. Right after the United States adopts the metric system. That is next on the agenda. Would we do it? I do not have that kind of pull. It is interesting to note, however, that this was proposed over a hundred years ago in a letter to the editor of the *New York Times*.[7]

Step 3: Get Our Hands Dirty

The last step is to look at the environment in our workplace with a process called 5S.[*] Anyone familiar with Lean will have taken part in 5S exercises in the past. They are dead simple and pay quick benefits to the team. They look like the depiction in Figure 2.1.

Pick any work area in the organization. We start in the 1 o'clock position with Sort.[†] Sort out the stuff that belongs here from the stuff that does not, two piles. Tell people the pile that does not belong will be donated or thrown out on Friday unless claimed. Most of it gets chucked. The stuff that is left over takes up about half the space.

Straighten out what is left; put it where it belongs. Articles or products that get used frequently are easier to reach or retrieve; others can be tucked away.

Shine can be a coat of paint, cleaning carpets, new lighting. Make the area look like something we are proud of people seeing and working around.

---

[*] The origin of 5S seems rooted in the works of Frederick W. Taylor (*The Principles of Scientific Management*, Harper & Brothers, New York, London, 1911) and Henry Ford (My Life and Work, Doubleday, Page, Garden City, NY, 1922), who were studied by Japanese managers. Indeed, Ford's CANDO program (Cleaning up, Arranging, Neatness, Discipline, Ongoing Improvement), which builds on Taylor's work, appears as the obvious origin for 5S. Source: Vital Enterprises http://www.vitalentusa.com. See also *Lean Methodology: Selecting and Executing a Personal 5S Application Project*, Darden Business, Charlottesville, VA, 2008.

[†] Also try this in your garage.

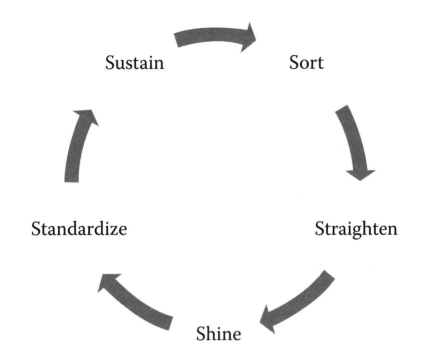

Figure 2.1 The 5S cycle.

Standardize is the way it stays. You can document it in process or customer-facing areas with photos and the appropriate procedures where necessary. Sometimes, we paint lines around where bins, machinery, and other pieces of equipment go. The lines signify a standardized layout and a systematic process: This is where that bin goes.*

Sustain is a cultural point. People need to be reminded not to drop unrelated stuff back into the area just cleaned.

I like to do this in a high-traffic part of the office or building first, which often turns out to be the area behind reception. People walk by there at least a couple times a day and will notice the improvements. In many cases, they will ask you to help them get started with a 5S in their work area. Post the before and after photos in the lunchroom or coffee room. It is a dead simple process that can enhance morale, improve a process, and free up space in your work area. We discuss in a further chapter what to do with that space.

---

* I worked with a program manager who went overboard with this with yellow tape around his computer, stapler, phone, and other paraphernalia on his desk. I respect his enthusiasm, but ...

Part of what I do with this last step is tell a story—think of it as Barry's management dyslexia: I look at it a bit backward. With 5S, we are demonstrating that someone is in charge, and someone cares. While I again connect seemingly unrelated concepts, Malcolm Gladwell did a great job describing the broken window theory in his book *The Tipping Point*.[8]* What does this have to do with 5S? Let us see.

The broken window theory talks about a situation where no one cares, and no one is in charge. Think about an area of your town that may be a bit run down. If someone breaks a window there and it is not fixed, the perception is that no one is in charge. Soon, more windows are broken, more litter is on the streets, and graffiti, drugs, and an escalation in crime soon follow. You have probably heard the analogy. The administration and the New York Police Department (NYPD) launched a major focus on the smaller "quality-of-life" crimes around the city: littering, graffiti, jumping turnstiles in the subway, urinating in public, and so on. Coupled with a greater presence of police officers and significant follow-up on various other initiatives around the city, New York saw a significant reduction in major crime over a short period of time. Someone was in charge, and someone gave a damn. Optics and visibility supported an effective execution of the new strategy.

In the same way, when we incorporate 5S, we show that we care about the work environment, and that someone is in charge. This is part of the relationship between responsibility and leadership. It is simple, but part of an awakening in perception, and the first step toward breaking paradigms and changing how we do things.

Lean does a few things for us in our drive toward innovation. The first step is freeing up the resources—people, space, time, money—in our environment to apply to innovative projects. If we do not have the people to implement the idea, there is no point in being more

---

* In their book, *Freakonomics* (HarperCollins, New York, 2005), Steven Levitt and Stephen Dubner countered that the reduction in crime could have more to do with the change in abortion laws and increased numbers of police officers than the broader strategies and efforts of the NYPD. Interestingly, major crime fell further, faster in New York City than other major cities that saw the same changes to abortion laws.

creative. The second step is more of a fundamental culture shift: When we start dealing with the complexity in our business, morale goes up. We are eliminating the processes and products that waste time, that frustrate customers, and that do not add value. In some cases, you will hear, "What took us so long?"

Finally, Lean environments often exhibit a sense of scarcity. That need or absence of excess can instill a sense of creativity[9] among the organization, as in the idea that if we cannot buy one, maybe we can make one. Scarcity of time forces us to be more efficient and creative with how we get things done. Companies have been successful by giving people back control of their time as an operating strategy. Customers of Netflix (discussed further in Chapter 6) keep several movies on hand as part of their subscription service for DVDs. This eliminates the need to pack up the kids in the car, drive to the movie rental store, pick out a movie, and drive home, freeing in some cases an hour of our time. As a result, movie watching becomes more spontaneous, and any night is "movie night." Part of the reason Netflix was successful with this strategy was because it realized people have less time than they used to for entertainment.

In the spirit of scarcity, consider what tasks we are responsible for or what meetings are on our agenda for the week. Which ones add no value? What could you do with that time if you could free up that time? What assets or expenditures do not add the value they used to or were intended to add? What could we do with the funds associated if we could eliminate these assets or expenditures?

Lean is an ongoing, long-term, full-time journey for the organization that takes it seriously. Many firms start the process and then abandon it because of the commitment it takes. As it builds momentum in the company, however, you can apply the resources from the Lean activities themselves toward further depth in Lean, or get them ready for *Next*, and the shift in your culture toward creativity and innovation. We look at a number of examples that combine Lean and innovation throughout the book.

I close this dialogue by recapping a discussion I had recently with a very senior member of the Canadian Armed Forces during one of our leadership programs at Queen's. He said, "I hear what you're saying, Barry, about Lean, and it makes sense. The problem I have is its reputation, and really, it's just boring. How do I get my people excited about it? Can we use another name?" He was right; Lean does have negative implications for some organizations. My response was, "How about *business process optimization* (BPO)? BPO is gaining traction in consulting practices. It sounds better. In fact, it sounds like something all of our companies could use. Who would not want their business processes to be optimized? Welcome to Lean. Dial down the complexity and waste, focus on the value that the customer is looking for, and your business processes are optimized. I am a simple guy, so I stick with Lean in this book. Maybe together we can give it back some sizzle.

The key point of applying Lean here is its role as an enabler in the organization. Section 2 of the book maps out the framework for our journey to *Next* in innovation, where Lean facilitates an agile approach to driving change.

A LEAN OPPORTUNITY: RESEARCH IN MOTION AND BLACKBERRY PRODUCT COMPLEXITY

The Canadian-based maker of Blackberry smart phones has fallen on difficult times of late. Competing products from Apple and Android-powered devices have taken significant market share; Samsung's Galaxy devices accounted for 23.8% of worldwide smart phone sales in the third quarter of 2011, Apple's iPhone was at 14.6%. Blackberry was not even in the top three in a category that it pretty much created not too long ago.[10] Investors suggested that the co-leadership of Mike Lazaridis and Jim Balsillie no longer works.* E-mail traffic through Research in Motion's (RIM's) server farms has been halted not once, but several times over the past several years, shutting down corporate and government Blackberry e-mail for a number of hours in each instance.

On the product side, it seems like more varieties of Blackberries enter the market every day. A recent report suggested there were

---

* In January 2012, Lazaridis and Balsillie stepped down as co-CEOs and were replaced by Thorsten Heins.

16 models available in Canada alone.[11] To get a sense for the impact of this product proliferation, we need to take a look at the stakeholders involved. More models means more shelf space required with the retailers; Best Buy would be reluctant to allocate more space to a brand that is suffering from volume decline. More model styles—keyboard, touch screen, flip—mean app developers have to modify their apps to work on multiple versions. Most apps[*] will not run in one format on all Blackberries, and fewer developers are willing to commit their time to doing that work for lower subscriber interest in their app. As of November 2011, there were over 500,000 apps for iPhone, 300,000 for Android, and less than 50,000 for Blackberry.[†] While few people would load more than a couple dozen apps on their phone, the availability of apps will have an impact on the consumers' handset decision.

Within RIM, the technical talent continues to split their efforts among many models and styles, instead of developing two or three devices that really grab the market's attention. Even packaging is different between models.

What about the most important stakeholder, the customer?

In our Starbucks example, we reflected on our first venture inside the coffeehouse and the anxiety we felt when considering the myriad options and choices. That was for a $4 beverage that will be gone in about 30 minutes. The bad decision risk for consumers with a cell phone is orders of magnitude higher.

Think about the last time you upgraded your cell phone.[‡] This is getting more complex as the capabilities of the phones go beyond what most of us will really use them for. Texting has grown exponentially, as has using a Web browser. Talking on phones has

---

[*] Applications; a "program" that performs specific tasks on a phone or computer, like pulling up today's copy of the *Wall Street Journal* or finding the closest Subway restaurant. Some apps generate fees and therefore revenues for the App Developer.

[†] Author's Web search. www.apple.com; www.pcmag.com; *Report: Android Market Reaches 500,000 Apps*, by Leslie Horn, October 24, 2011, http://www.pcmag.com/article2/0,2817,2395188,00.asp

[‡] Can we even call it a cell phone anymore? The purveyors of these products refer to them as smart phones, handhelds, and most recently I heard some devices labeled as *superphones*. That is just cocky to me. I am not sure what it does, but stopping bullets, flying, and leaping tall buildings are typical requirements of that moniker. My spell-checker certainly did not recognize it yet.

decreased. We download apps that customize our handheld based on personal preferences and information needs. GPS, good-quality cameras, MP3 music players, and games are all integrated into the same devices.

While the products themselves get more capable, retailers for cell phones get more plentiful. There are probably a half dozen kiosks in your local shopping mall selling them, while the carriers like AT&T, Verizon, and T-Mobile in the United States and Bell, Rogers, and Telus in Canada all have larger, more prominent footprints. Best Buy, Costco, Wal-Mart, and most other big retailers all sell them. All offer slightly different packages and pricing but agree that the more fine print we build into the agreement, the better.

Returning to RIM, suppose it narrowed down its product mix to two lines: a keyboard style consistent with the original Blackberries and a touch screen. Drop the seven Blackberry Curve models offered and three of the four Bolds. Delete the Pearl and its smaller keyboard with predictive text. Kill the Style flip phone; its screen is too small anyway for browsing. Eliminate the three Torches. Focus the development teams on one Bold (keyboard) and one Storm (touch screen). Keep things like security, something RIM is known for, at the forefront. Recognize that people want good browsers, cameras, and MP3 capability. Keep operational simplicity in mind—Apple sure does. And then, start asking questions about your customers: What else do they want? Where do they carry their phones? How can we make their lifestyles easier for them?

The answers to these questions certainly do not lie in offering more varieties of product models. Once we simplify but enhance user value, people will want the product again. A clear position in the market will attract users who appreciate that segment. App developers will write apps that work on Blackberries, drawing more consumers. Shelf space per model at Best Buy goes up, and their product experts push RIM again. RIM maintains some control with the carriers as a result of that end customer pull.

I was a long-time user of Blackberries, starting in the late 1990s with the basic black devices that really just managed e-mail and a calendar. I owned four or five different models over 12 years, but eventually moved to iPhones and then a Samsung Galaxy in 2011. They just plain do more, easier, although typing long or many e-mails can be a challenge. I have faith that RIM will get this figured out—I have friends in the company—but it will take some painful reflection and tough decisions to get there. More important, it will take a Lean, customer-focused approach to what is most important.

What do you really want or need in a cell phone?

CIRQUE DU SOLEIL AND LEAN INNOVATION

It is hard to view Cirque du Soleil as anything associated with Lean, but that is certainly how it started back in 1984. The troupe of 73 performers and employees started out with modest means, borrowing money from the Quebec government to fund the initial performances and equipment. When Cirque was invited to perform in the 1987 Los Angeles Arts Festival, there was barely enough money for a one-way ticket to California. If it had not succeeded, it would have had to leave its equipment behind and have the members hitchhike home. That type of beginning gets built into the fabric and culture of an organization. Guy Laliberté, long-time CEO of Cirque, said at the time, "I'd rather feed three acrobats than one elephant."[12]

Was the Cirque concept new in 1984? The package certainly was. Cirque evolved and expanded but stayed true to the concept of a circus without animals, yet built in a Broadway element. Lean, with Cirque, does not mean cheap or skimping on the show. At the core of the entertainment is the philosophy that, when the customer enters a Cirque Big Top, he or she will have an experience he or she will never forget. Acrobats and performers are recruited from around the world as the talent requirements for a series of shows that in 2009 entertained 15 million people[13] continue to expand.

Cirque is a combination of elements that were out there in the entertainment industry already: Montreal street performers, athletes from Eastern Europe with incredible strength and stamina, and Asian acrobats. Salt in a plot and a dose of sophistication for the clowns, and we have a show that we can charge a premium over previous

Cirque du Soleil	
Features we Lean out or Eliminate	Features we Enhance
• Animal acts, with the costs associated with handlers, trainers, veterinarians, transportation costs, food bills, and the guy following the elephant with a shovel • The Master of Ceremonies, announcing the Fabulous Linguine Brothers on the Flying Trapeze!	• The plot or storyline (in Italian, even) • Quality of entertainment (an experience we will never forget), with world-class performers • An image and market position closer to Broadway or Theatre

Figure 2.2 Cirque du Soleil.

circus models. Cirque was new, and not only have a lot of us seen a performance, almost all would say they would go again.

Figure 2.2 illustrates our Lean approach to innovation, and you will see this model several times through the book. On the left, the "thumbs down" highlights what we view as factors in the existing business model for the industry that can be reduced or eliminated, or "Leaned out." On the right, the "thumbs up" represents where we will expand our focus, using resources that may have otherwise been consumed by the factors in the thumbs down column. As discussed, Lean becomes the enabler for the organization, funding the key innovations in the new business model. Dr. Scott Sampson, a friend and professor at Brigham Young University, likes to say that Lean is as much about reallocating resources as eliminating waste.

In the end, Cirque's model is incredibly successful, with revenues of a half-billion dollars per year and millions of enthusiastic followers. Its ongoing commitment to creativity spawns new shows and venues, and even the occasional failure, as discussed elsewhere in this book.

NOTES

1. Christensen, C., *The Innovator's Dilemma*, Collins, New York, 1997.
2. Leung, C., "$10-million bulb," *Canadian Business*, p. 37, October 26, 2009.
3. Hamel, G., and Getz, G., "Funding growth in an age of austerity," *Harvard Business Review*, p. 5, July–August 2004.
4. Widely reported. See, for example, Grynbaum, M.M., "Starbucks takes a 3-hour coffee break," *New York Times*, February 27, 2008.
5. Perkins, T., "Old dogs, new tricks," *Globe and Mail*, February 25, 2011.
6. Levs, J., "Big 3 auto execs flew private jets to ask for taxpayer money," November 19, 2008, http://articles.cnn.com/2008-11-19/us/autos.ceo.jets_1_private-jets-auto-industry-test-vote?_s=PM:US.
7. Clarke, H.M., "Useless letters," *New York Times*, June 1, 1910.
8. Gladwell, M., *The Tipping Point*, Little, Brown, New York, 2000, p. 141.
9. Ott, A.C., "Invisible hand of time: how attention scarcity creates innovation opportunities," *Ivey Business Journal*, March/April 2011.
10. "Nokia Siemens plans to lay off 17,000 employees worldwide," *Globe and Mail*, November 24, 2011.
11. "RIM's model addiction," *Globe and Mail*, November 14, 2011.
12. Casadesus-Masanell, R., and Aucoine, M., *Cirque du Soleil—The High Wire Act of Building Sustainable Partnerships*, Harvard Business Review, Cambridge, MA, 2009.
13. Nelson, J., "Cirque's midlife crisis," *Canadian Business*, May 10, 2010.

2

Driving Innovation

3

The Innovation Framework

First comes thought; then organization of that thought, into ideas and plans; then transformation of those plans into reality. The beginning, as you will observe, is in your imagination.

Napoleon Hill, author

One of the things I discovered at a business school is that every theory eventually evolves into a framework. Business professors like frameworks almost as much as they like 2 × 2 diagrams. Perhaps there is a framework for creating 2 × 2 diagrams (in which case, we may like frameworks more than 2 × 2 diagrams, but that is starting to sound like the whole chicken-and-egg thing), although none of my colleagues has shared such a framework with me.

The purpose of the framework is to tie together the concepts of a theory in a pattern that makes the theory easier to explain, manage, and relate to our business needs. It can organize thoughts or provide a process to follow for the actual work. It becomes an anchor or foundation we return to as we navigate the improvement to our business supported by that structure. Frameworks come in many forms: recipes like my friend Jason's flank steak,* the 5S model in Chapter 2, or the innovation framework discussed in this chapter.

---

* Flank steak is a very lean cut of meat, great for healthier diets but tougher without some preparation. Marinate the steak in a mixture of soy sauce, teriyaki, brown sugar, and other spices for at least 24 hours. Cut the steak across the grain into strips about ¾-inch thick and fold the strips onto wooden skewers you have soaked in water. Grill the skewers on the barbeque grill for about 10 minutes for medium rare and enjoy.

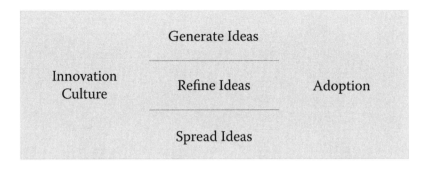

Figure 3.1 The innovation framework.

When I looked at some of the other work on innovation, I struggled with the idea of a *process* for innovation. Many of the current works on innovation discuss blueprints, tool kits, and steps for innovating in our companies. What I want to achieve is a framework *without* a process, negating the need for you to do everything we discuss in this book, contrary to conventional wisdom. You can thin slice this framework if you need to—each component can stand on its own. If the section on organizational culture is most relevant for you, take it away. For some of you, your firm already gets a lot of ideas, but refining the ideas to give you a fresh perspective is what you need, so see Chapter 6. In that way, my hope is that the framework itself is applicable to a broader audience rather than something locked into six steps or a blueprint.

Figure 3.1 is what the innovation framework looks like. Each section of the framework stands on its own but also supports the rest of the structure. We focus on the culture of the organization: Who drives the culture? What is our culture? Where does the culture come from? Is ours an innovative culture? Defining this is a challenge for any leadership team, but we find that most of our firms operate in a culture driven toward efficiency rather than creativity. We need both, but how do we do that?

In the subsequent section, we discuss the elusive ideas: Where do they come from? What happens to new ideas in our firm? Do we even get new ideas or understand that a new idea is in front of us? We also look at three tactics I have employed to generate ideas.

The difficulty with most ideas we develop is that they will not be sufficient in their initial state, call it the version 1.0 of the idea. Version 1.0 ideas are destined to die a horrible death at the hands of our competitors, the market, or even the devil's advocates in our conference room. The naysayers are everywhere. They are afraid of what is new and how it can upset their equilibrium. Version 1.0 ideas need to be *refined* and developed if we hope to launch them successfully. Chapter 6 discusses refining those ideas in depth.

Once we have refined the ideas to a form that is more applicable, it is about getting the ideas out there. Spreading the ideas is as much about executing the project that launches the idea as about how we set up the organization to pursue those ideas when we think we are ready. We spend time on both areas of focus.

In Chapter 8, we circle back for another discussion on driving an innovative culture because, in the end, our innovation process starts and ends with our culture. If we are serious about it, we need to be willing to change in the interest of driving to *Next* in our business.

This is not a complicated model. In fact, it is intended to be practical and straightforward. Simple, however, does not mean easy. Maybe the best way to highlight that is with another story. I forget where I heard this one, but it has always seemed like a great example of *simple* and *culture* to me.

Perhaps 10 years ago, the Physics 101 program at an East Coast university (call it ECU) was struggling. You may remember your experience with Physics 101: the giant textbook (we called ours the Green Monster), the class with 300 people in it, the professor who faced the blackboard the whole lecture and did not turn around once. I got through the course at my university, I think, with a B- and was quite happy with the result at the time. Well, the Science Department at ECU was concerned. In recent years, it had seen the failures for Physics 101 increase to an alarming level. On average, a third of the students taking first-year physics were failing and having to repeat the course or change programs. Situations like that build on themselves, and students entering the program hear the legends and are anxious from Day 1.

The Science Department looked at its course to see if there was something it could do. The curriculum was consistent with other university entry-level physics courses. The text was the same. There was nothing challenging about the lecture halls compared to other schools. The professors teaching the course were well respected and got decent evaluations. The quality of students being admitted was strong. So, what was up?

One of the professors suggested they try an experiment the next semester. The ad hoc committee agreed, so he took both sections of 300 students for the course, totaling 600 students. In the first section, he introduced the course the same way he had in the past (e.g., here is the syllabus, the text, my contact information, these are the expectations …). He went on to do an introductory discussion in physics, and then to wrap up the first class, he said something like, "Now, I know you've heard this is a tough course, and yes, it is. But study hard, ask lots of questions, and come and see me if you need help. I'm sure you'll do fine."

In the other section of 300 students, he started off just the same, including the introductory physics lesson. His wrap up, however, was very different. Here is what he said: "Now, I know you've heard this is a tough course, but I'm optimistic. I'm not sure how we did it, whether it was the Registrar's Office or the Science Department administration, but somehow we've got some of the best and brightest students in this class that I've ever seen. I've looked at your backgrounds, and I'm very excited about what we'll be able to do together this semester. Good luck!" That was it. The approach to both sections after that was exactly the same.

The results were very telling. Section 1 finished the semester similar to other recent groups who took the course, with about 30% of the students failing and having to repeat the course. Section 2? None of the students had to take the class over, and all the professor had done was to subtly alter the culture in that classroom to one of expected success from one of anticipated difficulty.

Simple, but not easy. Carry on …

COOL IDEAS: SAUNDERS FARMS*

What would you do with a 100-acre farm? Most grain crops would generate about $40,000 in top-line revenues on 100 acres. Livestock like cattle may get you closer to $60,000. In either case, it is hardly enough to get by on once you pay the expenses and feed the family.

Some of this went through the minds of Bill and Anne Saunders back in 1974 as they bought the plot of land about 30 minutes from downtown Ottawa, Ontario, Canada, now a city of almost 1 million people. Within a couple years of buying the farm (literally), they began a pick-your-own strawberry plot that eventually grew to about 25 acres. The experimentation continued as the focus on strawberries decreased, and a tree nursery was planted. This evolved further into hedge mazes and pumpkin patches and eventually what the Saunders refer to as "agritourism," or a destination farm. The Saunders brought in and reconstructed a number of heritage log cabins and older structures from around Ontario. They created a Fall Festival to celebrate the fall colors in Canada (and sell pumpkins). And, Saunders Farm is now home to the largest collection of hedge mazes in North America (Figure 3.2).

Is it working? In 2006, Saunders Farm attracted 80,000 visitors, including busloads of schoolchildren, families, and companies holding corporate retreats. Guests pay an entrance fee to get in and often buy pumpkins in the fall at a cost of $8 to $15 each (about double what a pumpkin costs at your grocery store), and they are quite happy to do it. "Farm revenues" are now north of $1 million per year.

What could you do with 100 acres? Perhaps something like what is discussed next.

COOL IDEAS: NOBLE CROP SCIENCE AND INNOVATION

Coming soon to a plate near you: For hundreds of years, the world's oldest profession's predominant focus on development involved increasing the yields of a crop per acre of land—more crop on less

---

* http://www.saundersfarm.com.

Saunders Farm	
Features we Lean out or Eliminate	Features we Enhance
• Livestock, including related shelter, food, vaccination, and care • Most crops, including related seeding and harvest equipment • Dependency on weather for seeding and harvest	• Entertainment, in the form of hedge mazes, heritage buildings, and festivals • Corporate retreat facilities • Pumpkin sales

Figure 3.2 Saunders farm.

land meant more food, more revenue at the market, and less time on a steer or tractor at harvest. Early focus on yield meant farmers selected the best grains from a crop and kept the seeds, using them the following year to initiate the next crop.

In the last century, farmers and scientists working together developed pesticides that kept weeds and insects at bay, increasing overall yields and the predictability of a crop, although costs increased through the purchase of spraying equipment, the pesticides themselves, and the time and fuel associated with spraying the crop.

Other challenges evolved for the agriculture community and policy makers as well. Land has become more valuable for development purposes, and cities and populations have grown, resulting in a difficult paradox: More food is required to support the increasing population, yet less land is being farmed.* Demand from foreign markets such as Asia exacerbates the problem. Solving such macro-level issues will take a variety of solutions and a lot of time, but what if one opportunity has been on the shelf already for 20 years?

---

* This is an appropriate place for regulation and its impact on development discussed previously. The role of the government and planners should be to allocate land use with a balanced perspective on uses and the needs of the population.

In an odd bit of serendipity, I met Garry Hoekstra on a train to Toronto in the fall of 2011. Garry has a PhD in agriculture science, is an agronomist (meaning he breeds plants), and is one-half of the duo heading up Noble Crop Science and Innovation with his partner, chief executive officer (CEO) Pierre Cadieux. Noble Crop's innovation (it is hoped the first of many) is a new strain of oat for the poultry and cattle feed market. Sounds boring, right? Think again.

The challenges with the traditional feed market are similar to those of the typical cash crop: Land costs are increasing; pesticides for new pest-resistant bugs and weeds are more expensive. Feeds themselves are getting more expensive. Corn and soybean meal—the current preferred feeds for livestock—are in greater demand in other markets, on the supply side of the biofuel market for corn (where it is subsidized) and health food for soybeans. Not only are we losing farmland to urban sprawl, but crops are also being diverted to power our cities and vehicles. As demand goes up, the price of animal feed goes up, the result being partially responsible for some of the increase you see in the price of meat in the supermarkets. As the population of the planet recently topped 7 billion, the combination of factors at play here is a significant issue.

What Garry Hoekstra has refined and bred through several generations of test and trials is what is called VAO-Oat: a hull-less oat ideally suited for the feed market. It is higher in protein and energy than corn or soybeans. It requires no pesticides and grows in more difficult locations where less-robust crops will not work. It is a good rotation crop, replenishing nutrients in the ground for other crops while earning farmers better returns than traditional rotation crops such as potatoes and especially summer fallow, where the grass is plowed back into the soil to rejuvenate it. The animals like it, in the agriculture version of the Pepsi challenge, and they gain weight faster. Laying hens produce eggs faster. Apparently, the meat from animals fed VAO-Oat tastes the same and is easier to cut. The nutritional value is the same. And, while enhancing the value curve in all the ways mentioned, it costs less to produce per ton.[1]

This sounds like a disruptive innovation to me. Interestingly, the Lean part of this innovation is that the first version of the seed for

VAO-Oat was on the shelf in Agriculture Canada's Seed Bank for 20 years, and no one realized its potential in the market.

The new oat is approaching the commercialization stage, but there are still some challenges ahead for Noble Crop. I have talked about the paradigms we all have, and farmers can be especially set in their ways. The key here is Noble Crop educating its customers on the opportunities associated with VAO-Oat. Corn and soybeans have been the traditional feeds for livestock for long enough that there is some resistance to change in the market. Hoekstra and Cadieux are driving the adoption process here with test plots where they demonstrate the ease with which the grain grows. They are working with cooperative partners, larger well-respected farmers whose opinions matter and carry some weight in their "field" (pun intended). Marketing will be key as well.

In addition to a high potential crop, what Garry has developed is a new breeding system for the grains, and it needs to be emphasized that these are not genetically modified plants. He breeds strains of plants together to get the best genes from the plants to come together in the final product. The potential is immense: a process driving lower-cost, higher-value feed that in effect shortens and enhances the food chain. At the time of writing, the partners had just signed a joint development agreement with McGill University's Agriculture Department and the National Science and Engineering Research Council (NSERC). In addition to funding, this agreement gives the duo access to expanded lab facilities and significant computing horsepower, allowing Garry to more effectively screen VAO-Oat varieties. This "marker-assisted" selection process helps Noble Crop identify the highest potential strains without waiting for test crops to be grown, essentially refining the innovation on a computer. Hoekstra's test-and-refine phase is consequently accelerated, taking months rather than years, getting the best strain "production ready" that much sooner.

Exciting Stuff! I sincerely wish them the best of luck.

NOTE

1. Author interviews with G. Hoekstra and P. Cadieux.

4

Innovation Culture

Why do we need to kill two birds with one stone? Was there a shortage of stones somewhere? Someone said, "You need to kill two birds with that stone."

Nick Thune, comedian

Let us flash back to the three firms discussed in Chapter 1 for a moment.

- Company A understands that it needs to change and be innovative on an ongoing basis to be competitive. This is a continuing process for the company and part of its culture.
- Company B appreciates the need for innovation, but the economy or industry factors are not right at this time. It does not believe it has the resources to innovate and is focusing on managing today's business.
- Company C would also like to be more innovative but does not possess the skill set necessary to drive "what's next" in its business.

If we look at how most of us are "wired," I think we would agree that many of us operate like Company B as individuals. We are all busy, overscheduled with meetings, tasks, activities for our kids after school, and deadlines. Multiple projects overlap each other, and we somehow manage to keep all the balls in the air. That balancing act, in fact, becomes a source of pride for some of us. The problem is, it is the wrong balancing act.

Figure 4.1 Efficiency versus creativity.

We have no downtime, no release from the pressures of that schedule that allows us to take a step back and think or reflect. We are bombarded with e-mails and texts 24/7 and are expected to stay plugged in.* Our smart phones now receive electronic copies of some of our favorite newspapers and magazines. The in-box is always full, which means the quality of the outbox deteriorates to a series of bullet responses, instructions, and updates. Our days lack creativity because we have no time for it.[†]

How can we have the time, however, if we do not take the time? The necessary evolution is a recognition within the organization that innovation and creativity *deserve* our support as leadership. Take a look at Figure 4.1: Which side of the picture indicates how your firm would spend most of its time and energy?

For most of us, the scales are tipped to the left. Realistically, when do we get time to think? I saw a clip recently of a firm that was developing a device capable of allowing us to get our text and Web updates in the shower, one of the last places where we truly get a few moments to ourselves. Say good-bye to the whole concept of thoughts in the shower.

I ask the following of every group I get to spend some time with in class or as part of a program: "How many of you are creative?" Typically, about 10% raise their hands. We talk about the things that represent their creativity: They draw or write, do photography or

---

* How many of us could get away with not carrying a cell phone? Could you make a statement that long-term balance in your life is more important than short-term accessibility?

† Some ideas for dealing with the pressures on our schedule are discussed in the final chapter.

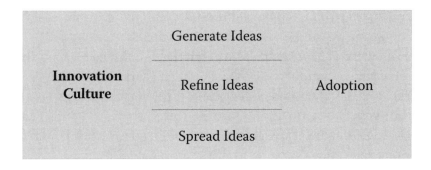

Figure 4.2 Focusing on culture.

woodwork, or they garden. "Excellent. Now what about the rest of you?" The feeling is that some of them do not have a creative bone in their body; their partners buy their clothes and dress them in the morning. Drafting a memo is a painful process, let alone a speech or a talk to a group of customers or employees. Good luck in the kitchen if the food did not come out of a box. They are highly efficient, yes, but not creative. At least that is what they think.

We touched on this briefly in Chapter 1. In most cases, that creativity is still there; it has just been beaten out of us. We are born curious, and curiosity is part of being creative. We ask a question, learn something, and use that knowledge to do something we could not do before.

In an innovation culture (Figure 4.2), we change our routines, talk to new people, and try something we have not tried before in our professional and personal lives. When we pick up the remote tonight, we try watching the nature channel on TV rather than the news. We see, for example, that lionfish now inhabit most reefs in the Caribbean Sea, when 10 years ago there were none in that part of the world. How did they get here? It turns out that they are native to Indo-Pacific, and pet stores brought them over to North America because they are a very pretty fish, and they were very profitable. People bought them and brought them home to their large 60-gallon aquariums, gave them a name ("Killer", probably, or maybe "Simba") and watched in horror as they killed the other fish in the tank. ("Oops, I wasn't expecting that. We paid a lot for those other fish.") So, if we are inland at all from the coast, we remove Simba and restock the tank.* If we are near the ocean, we release Simba back to the wilds "where she belongs," like the coast of Florida. Oops again. It turns out that lionfish have a voracious appetite and no natural predators other than sharks in this part of the world. They lay thousands of eggs at a time, and those eggs float in the currents for hundreds of miles. In a few short years, lionfish have migrated throughout the Caribbean, are taking over the reefs, and are on every scuba diver's and naturalist's "most hated" list.

As you are watching that show, you start off thinking: "Wow, this is interesting." Then you put your business hat on and think, "They have no natural competition in this market. Lionfish didn't come out of an R&D lab somewhere; they were brought here. They were introduced into this market from somewhere else, and now they own the space. How could my company do that?"

Aha. Okay, maybe it is an "aha moment," or maybe it is not. Interestingly, nature has several examples of human's influence upsetting equilibrium and "markets" are dominated by the newcomer.† The purpose of the analogy is to help us understand that until we start behaving and acting differently, the outcomes will stay the same. We will continue to be too busy to be creative. Until the organization supports a change in our routine or some downtime to think differently, the results will be the same. We will be busy, perhaps execute very well, but question our ability to innovate. This is a top-down decision where leadership (you) recognizes the importance of *Next*, and that without *Next*, today will be over pretty quickly. This is Company B evolving to Company A.

You may be familiar with 3M's strategy of encouraging employees to innovate on company time, the 15% rule. 3M leadership wants its employees at all levels to spend 15% of their time working on noncore projects, that is, initiatives of their own outside their day-to-day activities. This 15% time allocation is regarded as critical in achieving their growth objective, where 40% of sales should come

---

* With a few harsh words to the pet store employees for not warning us about the predatory nature of the lionfish.
† Look up the weed purple loosestrife or the zebra mussel infestation. Both were native to other parts of the world, brought to North America, and are now dominating wetlands and the Great Lakes, respectively.

from products or services developed in the last five years. This is not a new initiative—it has been part of 3M's culture for decades, and it is jealously guarded even in recessionary times.[1] You know this is part of the culture when employees come in on a Saturday to work on that personal project,* and the wildly successful Post-it Note product is a great example of that initiative.

Google does something similar; engineers are expected to devote 20% of their time to projects of their own initiative. On top of the guidelines, however, is the work environment at Google, with foosball and pool tables, slides going down between floors, couches and recreational areas for kicking back and what may be perceived as goofing off in a lot of companies. Google Earth, G-mail, and other products have come out of the commitment to downtime for employees at Google.

Whether your company sets formal guidelines like a 3M or a Google or you dedicate resources to innovation and creativity, support for the process needs to be woven into the fabric of the organization. Your employees do not need a PhD to have a good idea. We challenge ourselves because our customers challenge us and expect more. We are willing to try things, knowing full well that we will fail more often than not, but we will learn something in the process that makes us better. Most important, we understand that to succeed, an organization needs to refresh, reset, and develop continually, and never be satisfied with the status quo.[2]

That is an innovation culture, and given its importance to innovation in general, we spend more time on culture in Chapter 8 to wrap up the book.

DN101 LIGHTING PROGRAM AND INNOVATION CULTURE: APPLYING THE INNOVATION FRAMEWORK

I spent a number of years working for a private automotive parts manufacturing company in Canada called Autosystems. This was a great

---

* Work–life balance discussions are important to me with this concept. Part of company culture needs to recognize the trade-offs with committing to a project on a weekend. That employee should have no issue, for example, taking off early on Wednesday to coach his or her child's Little League team.

organization, and one I refer to several times throughout this book. I was part of a small, young, and enthusiastic management team led by a man named Don Warren; the team grew the business from scratch to about $200 million in sales. In many cases, we had no right doing some of the things we were doing or trying some of the things we were trying, but it was a culture of solving our customers' problems. In business, sometimes we say "yes" and then figure out how to do it.

In 1995, we received a call from Ford Motor Company regarding a program we had launching with them later that year for the new model of the Ford Taurus (DN101 was Ford's code name for that Taurus), one of their highest-volume vehicles. If you look inside today's headlamp assemblies, you will usually see a shiny silver unit inside that guides the light forward from your vehicle in a pattern that optimizes how well you see at night. That component is called a reflector. One of our facilities made these reflectors for customers like Ford, GM, and others, and the Taurus program was going to be large: 600,000 vehicles per year or 1.2 million reflectors (two headlamps and reflectors per vehicle). The Taurus reflector was quoted to Ford to cost about $3 each, so the program was worth close to $4 million per year, which is not bad business.

Ford's lighting group, however, had a problem. New headlamp designs were creating challenges for engineers in how to assemble the components, especially in a high-volume program like that for the Taurus. Ford's people threw in the towel and asked if we could take on a larger role and assemble some neighboring components to our reflector and ship that subassembly to Ford rather than just the reflector. When we evaluated the assembly, it certainly was not what you would call a no brainer. They had designed a rubber skirt to fit between our reflector and the mating headlamp housing at the back of the lamp and had no way to bond the skirt to the reflector. There needed to be a watertight seal between the skirt and the reflector to prevent water from getting into the back of the headlamp, where it could condense on the inside of the lens. That condensation looks bad and affects performance.

By the way, start of vehicle production (Ford's Job 1) was only a few months away.

Innovation Culture

Our project manager at the time pushed back, being concerned with our ability to solve the assembly issue and still launch the program successfully. It certainly was a risky situation. Our product line with Ford at the time also was purely headlamp reflectors, and adding assembly could take away from that focus. Don Warren accepted the challenge, however, and allocated additional resources to the project.

Generating Ideas

We called in some of our best suppliers (including 3M, interestingly) to look at the various adhesives they had available. Testing began on a number of different iterations of the assembly. Concurrently, manufacturing engineers began the design and build of the assembly cell to put the components together. With over a million units required per year, the cycle time needed to be around 15 seconds per part. In generating ideas, we looked at some new presses, ovens, and curing processes that could get an adhesive to bond the skirt to the reflector. We tried mechanical clips as well, mounted to the outside of the reflector and skirt, holding the two together while the adhesive cured.

Refining Ideas

The manufacturing process went through a series of refining iterations, each one addressing the manufacturing weaknesses realized in the ongoing product testing while building on the strengths of earlier concepts. This seemed like trial and error, but each failure led to new knowledge, improvements, and zeroing in on the target. The first version evolved to second- and third-generation assemblies very quickly. The fixed deadline for start of production and the volume of the program itself put significant pressure on the team to solve the issues. While we were solving these assembly issues, the engineers at Ford kept adding more components to our assembly: a leveling device to aim the headlamp, a bracket to hold the level, rivets to hold the bracket. Our scope increased as Ford became increasingly confident we could solve the problems that their people could not or did not have time for.*

Spreading Ideas

As the ideas spread, there were some temporary negative cost aspects to the final assembly, which we were able to Lean out later as the production and volumes settled down, but the average selling price for Autosystems on this program rose from just over $3 to around $15 per assembly. Volumes increased somewhat as well, and what started as a $4 million program became almost $20 million per year.

The final version of the assembly utilized a thermally cured adhesive to bond the skirt to the reflector, resulting in the need for a high-temperature tunnel on the assembly line. As the assemblies emerged from the tunnel, the joint between the skirt and reflector was pressurized to test for leaks in line, all at a cycle time of four parts per minute.

Adoption

Had we said "No" to Ford when it came to us with its challenge, as a couple of people on the team suggested, and focused just on our reflector, we would have missed out on a huge opportunity. These challenges stretched our thinking and capability, broke paradigms, and made the organization better as we drove to adoption of the reflector assembly. Autosystems demonstrated that we were willing to think, try, and occasionally fail, and it was because of this that Ford and others continued to rely on the organization to solve problems like the Taurus lighting program.

NOTES

1. From a conversation with Jim McSheffrey, managing director of 3M UK PLC.
2. Manyika, J., "Google's view on the future of business: an interview with CEO Eric Schmidt," *McKinsey Quarterly*, p. 1, September 2008.

---

* Our labor costs were far lower than theirs as well, so some of this was cost motivated. Again, there is the negative impact of organized labor on innovation in certain work cultures.

5

Generating Ideas

Learning and Innovation go hand-in-hand. The arrogance of success is to think what you did yesterday will be sufficient tomorrow.

William Pollard, author and clergyman

Where do ideas come from in your firm? As important, what happens to ideas in your firm?

We touched on research and development (R&D) in Chapter 2 as a source for ideas in many firms. Our focus here, however, is on simpler means, those requiring less heavy lifting. The new knowledge coming out of R&D is essential, but I prefer not to lay responsibility for innovation at the feet of one department.

In 1985, management guru and business professor Peter Drucker wrote *Innovation and Entrepreneurship*,[1] one of the earlier works connecting innovation and leadership. Drucker talked about other sources of ideas beyond R&D, sources that required more awareness of what was going on around us than investment in a lab and PhDs to run it. Specifically, he used terms like

- The unexpected
- Incongruities
- Process need
- Changes in perception

This is where Lean and innovation come together. Professors W. Chan Kim and Renée Mauborgne[2] have referred to it as a recombination of existing elements or products and services from other business lines that we bring together to make changes in our business, such as with Cirque du Soleil. Next we discuss two other examples, one real and one on the way (it is hoped).

The smart folks at Proctor and Gamble (P&G) brought us Crest Whitestrips several years ago in the interest of whitening society's teeth. Maybe you have seen them or perhaps used them. Whitestrips are a film coated with a paste containing hydrogen peroxide in a concentration of around 5% or 6%, depending on which version you use. It is a very simple system; you just peel open the envelope, pull the strips off the backing, and apply them to your top and bottom teeth. Whitestrips cover your front six teeth, typically what you see when a person lights up the room with their smile. You wear the strips on your teeth for 30 minutes and then remove them and throw them away. Repeat for two weeks and you should have whitened your teeth by a couple of shades.

Do they work? It appears so. P&G created the "home whitening" market, a market now worth about $250 million a year, and Crest Whitestrips products control about half of it.[3]

Our perception here is that a lot of R&D must go into products like this. In reality, however, this one took less heavy lifting than we might think. The ingredients for this innovation were already in P&G's stable. While the lab folks in the white coats may vehemently object, what they basically did was take a bleaching agent from their detergents division and combined it with film from their paper products division[4]: The idea was to "put them together and see if we can get someone from 'upstairs' to try it out. After all, we can't try this stuff out on animals."

Okay, I am stretching it a bit. The testing of a product like this is very extensive, and P&G is not the type of company to take shortcuts with people's health. The idea, though, was right there. It was taking concepts, products, and services from different parts of its business, combining them in ways not done before, and here we are. There is the novel solution, and generating the idea was easier than thought. Hats off to P&G for its creative thinking.

What if we can do that with products or services from outside our business? How about a refrigerator that talks to you? (Some of you are saying that your refrigerator already talks to you. In fact, it seems to *call* to you on occasion.) Home appliances can struggle for inclusion in any category considered "cutting edge." For many years, innovation in this area meant a new color or texture to the surface of your fridge (remember avocado green?). Then, we started looking at energy-wise appliances. Integrated ice makers and water dispensers have been around for years. Freezers are now designed on the bottom of the appliance rather than the top. About 10 years ago, there was the ill-fated integration of a small TV set into the front of a refrigerator. But, what about really adding some functionality to your appliances that helped manage your day?

Let us say you are on your way home from work, and your fridge sent you an e-mail. As your smart phone vibrates, you break off the conversation you are having with your neighbor on the train and look down. You say, "Sorry, it's my fridge. I need to take this." You read the screen, and it appears that you are out of orange juice, and the milk is about to go past the "best before" date. There are also a half dozen other items you need to pick up on the way home after you get off the train.

Would that be a helpful feature? I have been talking about this example for a couple of years, and the response to the idea has been strongly favorable. What would it take? Well, we would need some way of reading the key data on some of your core groceries. Radio-frequency identification (RFID) tags have been out for years, and the passive versions cost three cents to five cents each—they are cheap. We could store volume (two liters of milk), type (you like 1%), and expiry date on the RFID tags. We would also need some way of reading the tags. An RFID sensor inside the fridge, wired to the Wi-Fi unit we will build into the fridge would have an additional cost of about $30. On your home computer, we build a grocery list program where you keep your basic household needs: milk, juice, eggs, maybe beer. It may be tough to get vegetables and fruit on there, but you are restocking those on a weekly basis anyway. The grocery list program is created by the appliance company, downloaded over the Internet.

So, we add $30 in cost to the fridge. The company that develops and launches the first real "smart fridge" can probably charge an extra $500 for it, and people will pay. There are options on how we get the RFID tags on the groceries. The stores could do it as a value-added option; the appliance manufacturers could supply you with a package of reusable RFID tags that you could program at home. I really think, however, that the grocery suppliers and retailers would get together on this and do it for you from the factory. It adds a bit of cost but will help in inventory control, and they would just mark the item up a few cents anyway.

Take it a step further. You are running late, and the kids are hungry—no problem. Send a text to your oven: "Turn on. Setting: bake. Temperature: 425 degrees." In 15 minutes, you are home, the oven is hot, and you can throw the frozen pizza in the oven. Maybe it is not safe to turn on the oven when you are not home, so we will have to think about that one. On the other hand, you will never have to turn around after just leaving the house because you think you may have left the oven on. Send it a text: "Turn off." What about an app that allows your smart phone to operate your TV and home entertainment system like a remote control* or start your car from inside when it is cold outside?

These products and functions are being developed as we speak by companies I have worked with. Will they take a ton of R&D? Not really. The toughest part will be getting companies that have not traditionally worked together to talk the same language. All we are really doing here is bringing together concepts, products, functions, and services from different industries and companies that have not been combined in the past. The key is that we are adding value for consumers. When we start to make their lives easier, they will get excited.

We return to your train ride: You put your phone away after reading the e-mail and look around. Your train buddies are staring at you with their mouths hanging open. One brave soul asks, "An e-mail from your fridge?" "Sure," you say. "It was telling me I'm

---

* How fast do these things change? This one is apparently coming out on iPhone now.

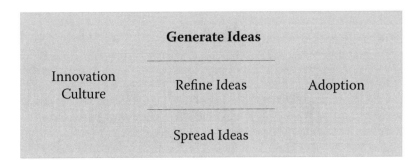

Figure 5.1 Generating ideas.

out of milk and juice, and there is only one beer in the fridge. It also reminded me the Lakers game is on TV tonight, so I may need some munchies." (You can add favorites and preferences to the standard grocery list, and the program can sync to ESPN. Now we're talking!) They are stunned. "Your fridge can do that?" "Sure," you reply. "It's my new SmartFridge. Don't you have one?"

How do we get ideas like that?

Ideas and innovations that result from those ideas can be externally focused (i.e., products or services that enhance the lives or experiences of our customers) or internally focused (improvements to our processes and systems that increase speed, reduce cost, etc.). Both sides are discussed here.

Let us return to our questions that led off this chapter. Where do ideas come from in your firm? What happens to those ideas (Figure 5.1)? This is an area that relies heavily on the culture we discussed in the Chapter 4, requiring commitment from leadership and some hard work by people throughout the firm. Many firms have submission processes for ideas, but many of those same firms will admit they do not work all that well. Ideas are submitted occasionally, but few are acted on. In some cases, ideas may indicate the firm's leadership is not as effective as it could be. Other ideas are not properly understood or presented. In most cases, however, the reason is connected to our busy and complicated work lives: Plain and simple, we are too busy to do anything with the ideas. Even if we could review them and agree that a few have merit, we really do not have the resources to refine and implement them.

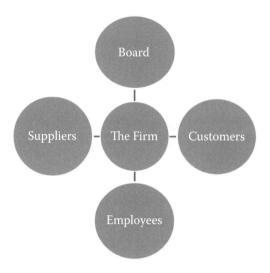

Figure 5.2 Idea sources.

Since we covered the resource discussion in Chapter 2, let us look now at the process for collecting and reviewing ideas. Where do the ideas come from? That could be anywhere, as long as we are listening (see Figure 5.2). Your suppliers are a terrific source of ideas, and they want you to succeed; when your firm wins, they win through more business. We used to do some business with 3M, and representatives from their firm would visit from time to time and leave products for us to try. A lot of times, we could not do anything with the product, but occasionally it solved an issue for us, and we were able to put it into play.

A board of directors or advisory board should be able to generate ideas based on their experience or other noncompeting organizations they work with, in addition to governance responsibilities. Two other great sources of ideas are the people who build your products or provide your services (employees) and those who use those products and services (customers).

I was booked on a flight in the spring with Air Canada and had a morning meeting in Toronto prior to the flight. The meeting wrapped up early, so I headed to the airport to get some work done before my flight. When booking the ticket online, I had the option of buying a day pass for the Maple Leaf First Class Lounge, but I did not bother as I had thought I would not have time to really take advantage of it.

So, arriving at the terminal, I went to the lounge and asked if I could buy a pass now. I was two hours ahead of my flight, and thought waiting in the lounge would be more effective than waiting in the main terminal. Sadly, it was not to be. The representatives looked quite indignant as they informed me that you cannot buy a pass to enter the lounge. When I explained that it was available online with my ticket purchase, the response was along the lines of, "Well, we don't do it on site." As I walked away, I could hear one attendant telling the other, "He tried to buy a pass to come in!" Shame on me.

Now, ignoring tone and customer service for a moment, this seems like an opportunity to me. How many passengers like me may want to pay a premium to rest or work more comfortably before a flight? From previous experience when I traveled more often and earned upgrades and free passes to the lounges, they are usually half empty (not half full; airlines are pessimistic businesses these days), so there is room. Worst case, we add a bit more revenue to the lounge on a quiet day. Best case, passengers like it there and choose to buy an annual membership or upgrade their flight the next time. Customer loyalty probably goes up as well. We cap the number of day passes we sell so the lounge is never overcrowded and affecting the service for our true first-class passengers. This seems simple enough to me. Based on the lounge attendant's body language, tone, and parting comment as I walked away, however, I am quite sure my encounter never spawned an idea submission within Air Canada's system. I generally appreciate Air Canada—the flights are on time, they go where I need to be, and their in-flight service is reasonable—but air travel is a very competitive business, and the airlines need every edge they can get. Are they listening to their customers? I do not think so.

Consider again our friends at P&G, who also invented the Swiffer, that great dust collection device many of us have in our homes now. The story has it that the reps from P&G first approached Wal-Mart about getting the product some shelf space in their stores. Wal-Mart looked at it, and said, "Can you put it on a stick?" This was an odd question, perhaps; at the time, the first-generation Swiffers were handheld devices. Wal-Mart's merchandise people, however, thought it would be great for cleaning ceiling fans and window blinds, so it needed to be on a stick. Now, Swiffers are available on a stick and work well not only on ceiling fans but also as brooms and dusters. P&G listened to its customers.

Listening to our employees gets more complicated as the organization grows. Many of you reading this book are part of companies employing hundreds or thousands of people. Collecting ideas in an effective manner for groups that size is a challenge. Think about the steps involved in an employee-driven idea program. First, employees need to know that you want their ideas. That is a leadership responsibility and, done well, embeds the process of collecting employee ideas into the culture of the company. If this is new for your firm, do not be shy about it. Broadcast it, celebrate it, and pump it up in employee meetings. Put posters on the walls and headers on the Web site telling the team you want their ideas. Also, tell them why (refer to Chapter 1 for some reasons if you need them).

Section 2 is a process for collecting those ideas. Some companies still use hard-copy written forms, especially in a plant environment, while many have taken this process online. Nothing fancy is required here: What is your idea? How would it work? What need or opportunity would it satisfy? Give people the ability to attach a sketch or diagram. The ideas should be submitted to at least a supervisor, but ideally to a central coordinator. Again, some companies make this a live person with responsibility to manage the flow of ideas and submissions, while others have automated it through standardized forms submitted in the company intranet* and distributed to the best-suited recipient based on the nature of the idea.

The next step is critical to maintain the momentum of the process: Someone needs to respond to the originator of the idea. It sounds simple, but the best way to kill an employee's enthusiasm for your process is to ignore his or her participation. The initial response should not take more than a week and can be very simple: "Thanks for your submission! A team will be reviewing it later this month." Some companies give the employee a gift of a hat or a coffee mug the first time he or she submits an idea to welcome the employee to the program.

---

* Intranets are Internet-like networks for sharing information and data among employees of a company and normally are inaccessible to outsiders.

Black and Decker Canada's Brockville facility used a program called FOCUS, for Focus on Cost and Unrealized Savings. Ideas were collected through the year but really saved for a two-week blitz on evaluating, testing, and implementing the ideas. Through most of the year, operations, new products, and other key initiatives were top on the agenda, but for those two weeks, everyone across the organization was part of the FOCUS team—simple, yet effective.

One company with a very interesting approach to gathering employee ideas is 1-800-Got-Junk, a Canada-based company that helps people get rid of the clutter in their basements, garages, and attics. In the lobby of its headquarters, there are a couple of whiteboards mounted to the walls. As employees walk in and out during the day, they can write their latest idea or thought on the whiteboard. Other employees walking by see the idea and add to it or build on it, creating an impromptu storyboard over the course of a couple of days. Team members download the history off the idea boards on a regular basis and discuss which ones they can take forward, which takes us to the next important step in an employee-driven idea process.

The final stage is a leadership review of the ideas that have been collected during the period. This should be a regularly scheduled event, with cross-functional representation from across the company. In the initial stages of the program, there may not be as many ideas, and you can tie this discussion into another meeting. As it grows, however, the idea review meeting becomes its own entity and is held at least monthly.

You will need to review the ideas against several criteria. While the criteria are dependent on your type of business, your vision, and your industry, here are some thought starters:

- Will it (the idea) enhance the customer experience?
- Will it save time, cost, or resources?
- Does the idea resolve a problem in our current processes?
- Does the idea fit our current vision or strategic agenda?
- Could the idea create a new vision or strategic agenda?

A yes or a maybe answer to any of these questions should lead to at least a further review of the submission. At that point, you assign

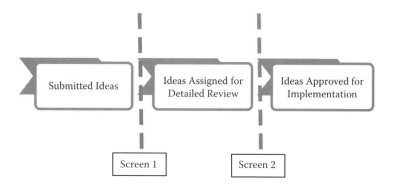

Figure 5.3 Idea review.

responsibility for a more in-depth review of the idea to someone in the organization and a date for appropriate follow-up. Whether the idea is pursued or not at this stage, it is important to again connect with the idea's originator. "We liked your idea and are digging into it further," or, "Unfortunately, we won't be able to pursue it, and this is why." Interestingly, in the Google and 3M worlds, employees go beyond the idea submission and start to refine the idea, testing and evaluating the idea into a working concept.

I like to use a model with two screens for idea submissions (see Figure 5.3). The first screen represents the meeting discussed previously, where submissions are reviewed for opportunity, fit to the business strategy, and so on. After the ideas are assigned and analyzed in more depth, the team gathers again for a review at Screen 2: Feasibility. Here, we look at whether we *can* do the idea; Screen 1 was about *should* we do the idea. The following questions support Screen 2:

- Do we have or can we get the resources to initiate this idea?
- Do the long-term benefits outweigh the short-term and long-term costs? (Sometimes this is a difficult consideration related to customer value.)
- Would the idea's potential launch timing fit the cadence of our project launches currently in the pipeline?

Once we have agreed that an idea has the merit to pursue, it essentially becomes a project. We will spend more time on this in Chapter 7, but the short version for now is that we assign responsibility to a team to fully develop and implement the idea. Sometimes this is a quick process, done with internal resources and a quick realization of benefit. In other cases, the idea and project are far more significant, requiring external expertise and potentially creating new opportunities for the company. Regardless, we are seeing the benefit of asking for ideas from employees and listening to customers. The moment some of these ideas are implemented, celebrate it. Reward employees for their ideas. Sometimes this is a monetary award or prize. In other cases, we reward people by putting them on the team that implements the idea and takes it to market.

One of the most effective idea processes I have been around was used by Magna, one of the largest automotive parts companies in the world. Each Magna division assigned an individual representative to gather the ideas from that division's employees and manage them through the process. There were enough ideas and submissions in most divisions that this was a full-time job. This person would collect the ideas as they were submitted and regularly meet with the submitting employee or employees to clarify and fine-tune the submission. He or she would then present those ideas to the leadership committee on a monthly basis. Many of the ideas would be rejected right away, but five or six would be assigned for further review at each meeting.

The really interesting part of the process with Magna was the reward for employees when their idea was implemented. Team members whose ideas led to additional revenues or cost savings totaling over $100,000 were invited to an annual gala. I attended several of these galas with Magna, and the last one had roughly 2,000 people in the room, representing all divisions of that branch of Magna. The gala was a semiformal affair, giving people a chance to dress up and eat a nice meal. There was entertainment: comedians, music, giant video screens all over the room with live feeds from around the banquet center. There were also prizes; the name of one person from each division was randomly drawn and awarded a check for $1,000, and one person in the hall went home at the end of the night with a new car.

Magna and its divisions spent about $2 million on that gala, but those in leadership still thought they were getting a deal. The ideas implemented by the people in the room totaled about $100 million, and the enthusiasm built by the gala and seeing people around them win cash and cars maintained the momentum for the program.

So, what happens to ideas in your firm? Do we ask for ideas? Do we recognize that without ideas, the firm will not grow, will not develop, and will not be able to fend off the competition? Do we appreciate that our customers, especially our future customers, expect us to be thinking about *Next*?

Asking for ideas is one thing, and a very good thing, but for firms just getting started in innovation, it is a difficult cultural transition. Sometimes, we can ask for and listen to ideas; other times, we need to go out and get them. With that in mind, I look at three tactical approaches to generating more ideas, creativity, and curiosity within the company.

CREATE AN *I-SPACE*

Back in Chapter 2, we discussed the benefits of freeing up space in the workplace; here is one of those opportunities. Creating an *i-space* is something I noodled around with a couple of Deloitte people in 2010 at their annual partner's meeting in Toronto. Have a look at the conference rooms and boardrooms around your office. If you are like most firms, they pretty much all look the same: nice, comfy chairs around a long table, a speakerphone in the middle, whiteboards on the wall. Maybe some plaques are on the wall to remind us how successful we are.

Next, think about the meetings you are engaged in several times a day in those rooms. People show up late. People are texting or e-mailing during the meeting; there are side-bar discussions. People sit in the same chairs every week following the same agenda. In most cases, our meeting culture is awful, and it is no wonder we struggle for new ideas in some of these meetings.*

So, why don't we create an environment that feels different to the people in it, that maybe makes them a little less comfortable but is still very functional? There is your *i-space*.† Take that same conference room and get rid of the chairs. Replace them with some funky chairs

---

* More on shaking up our meeting culture is given in Chapter 8.
† This is italicized because it seems that anything starting with an *i* in a sexy font or italicized letter instantly creates more credibility and cachet for the idea.

and stools from IKEA, with lots of bright colors.* On the end of the table, mount a roll of butcher paper and leave lots of Sharpie markers around to sketch or draw out the ideas. Just inside the door to the room, mount a shelf on the wall; this is where people set their phones when they come into the room (very uncomfortable for some, I will tell you). Underneath that shelf, put a shoe mat on the floor. This is where people leave their shoes when they come in the room (also uncomfortable, but interestingly, less of an issue than leaving a phone on the shelf). Lay down some very plush carpeting to reward the "no shoes" environment. Take down the plaques on the wall and leave the space for situational wall hangings; in some cases, these are customer sketches or processes related to the issue that is the focus; in others, use the wall space to hang the butcher paper filled with thoughts and ideas.

Companies do this in different ways, and in different orders of magnitude. Samsung's Value Innovation Program (VIP) utilizes a dedicated creative space that includes 38 bedrooms, a kitchen, and a workout room for extended stays.[5] Sir Richard Branson bought a castle in England and converted it for creative purposes at Virgin.

We can use the *i-space* (you have figured it out by now—the *innovation space*) for regular meetings in a pinch, but I like to save it for times when we need to get outside the box a bit. The room just feels different. People come in, leave their phones and shoes by the door, pull up a stool, and get at it.

Um, get at what, you say?

STORYBOARDING

Sometimes, you need to be able to force the development of an idea, and storyboarding† is one of my favorite ways to do it.[6] I was first introduced to storyboarding as an advertising tool in my first-year

---

* Apparently, the color green stimulates creativity, according to a study broadcast on CFOJ 95.5 FM, May 29, 2012.
† Storyboarding gets its name from the picture boards used to outline the story for an advertising campaign, animation, or video creation, and owes its roots to Walt Disney's first forays into animation in the 1930s.

MBA marketing course in 1991. Over the last 20-something years, it evolved into a problem-solving and innovation tool as well.

Most companies start here with brainstorming, and while there are exceptions, most groups do not brainstorm well. Think about the last time you were in a group idea process, say with 8 or 10 people. At one end of the scale are the people who are less comfortable speaking up and may not venture an idea. At the other end are people who are quite comfortable speaking up and offer many ideas. In examples of social Darwinism, people in the room will also tend to follow the lead (and ideas) of meeting bullies or those in the room who rank the highest. As ideas are suggested, they are discussed, often leading to long, tangential dialogues that consume significant time. You will also hear things like, "Yes, but … " or "We tried that a few months ago, and … ," despite an opening comment that "there are no bad ideas!"

The result of an hour's work is often a few ideas, certainly, but more ideas that have been killed or not offered at all. In that environment, it is easy to see why some firms do not believe they are creative or innovative.

Storyboarding resolves many of those issues, mostly by keeping the process anonymous and silent—no opinions, personalities, or negativity. Keep the group small, leave the phones at the door, and block off an hour for the activity. This can be done in person or virtually with some basic intranet programming. Queen's School of Business, for example, uses an electronic version of storyboarding in its Executive Decision Center (EDC). The process is popular; in 2011, the EDC ran 41 facilitations at Queen's and on the road with various clients.

The requirements for the analog version are as follows:

- 5 to 10 people, cross functional if possible
- Sharpie markers, black
- Masking tape
- 3 × 5 cards (about 100)
- Red and green stickers or Sharpies of those colors
- A problem, need, or opportunity
- A neutral facilitator

As the facilitator, distribute markers and 3 × 5 cards to the participants in the room. We start by defining the big hairy problem or opportunity that is the focus. The example I like to use is a new focus for a major hotel chain. The company has hotels in each major category, from budget hotels through the luxury group. In fact, the chain does quite well in the three- and four-star categories, with strong brands and good customer loyalty. Where it struggles, however, is in the budget category. In this group, it seems that all competitors offer the same service and facilities: a small but clean lobby, a small lobby restaurant or dining area, a pool, and a workout room with one or two treadmills. The rooms are reasonably spacious and clean, and the beds are okay. You have probably stayed at properties like this while on the road in a smaller town on business or perhaps with your family on a weekend. All of the chains offer this same hotel concept, which typically means that when more than one occupies the same area of a city, they compete on price. Therein is the core challenge for our hotel company: Their upper-category properties are doing fine, but the budget chain just breaks even or, more often, loses money.

We could focus on a cost-cutting initiative for that group or perhaps look at exiting that segment altogether. Cost cuts in a service business, as you would anticipate, often lead to a reduction in service for customers and therefore fewer customers staying at the hotel. Exiting the segment creates problems as well; customers who are part of the loyalty program get points and rewards for staying at any of the properties, including the budget line. If we do not offer properties in the budget segment, customers will stay with another chain when they need a lower-priced option or are in a location we no longer serve. The odds are if they are happy with their stay at the competing chain, they will stay with it more and with us less.

There must be a better way, thus creating the topic for our storyboarding exercise. Your task, group, should you choose to accept it, is to develop a new concept for a budget hotel chain. We put a short form of the problem or opportunity in the header card on your white board or easel, which we call the Opportunity Card (see Figure 5.4). Following the Opportunity Card, we have our Focus Cards, which

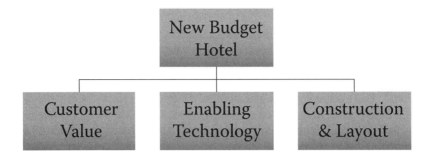

Figure 5.4 Storyboarding header layout.

frame the opportunity and keep us focused on the challenge itself. In most cases, I let the group develop the Focus Cards based on industry experience, customer input, or resource expertise. In this case, I will set the Focus Cards, as you will note in Figure 5.4. First, what does the customer want? What does the customer really value or need in a budget hotel chain? This also extrapolates into what the customer does not want or need. Second, how could technology support this new chain? What would technology enable or restrict in operating the facilities or managing the customer experience? Last, how would we build the place? What would the layout look like? How would we furnish it?

With this on the board, the participants get at it. Tell them you are looking for just a few words on each card, not a paragraph, picture, or long explanation. One to four words is best. Write big and clearly with the black Sharpies. When participants write a paragraph or long description of their idea, the writing needs to be smaller, and it becomes difficult for other team members to read. As Idea Cards are filled out, the neutral facilitator collects the cards, and once he or she has a decent number, starts taping them on the board. I like to have a number of one-inch sections of masking tape already torn off and lightly taped to the edge of the board. Push pins and a corkboard work just fine as well.

Each Idea Card you collect gets assigned to one of the categories. This is not a foolproof process, so we do not worry too much if a card overlaps a couple of Focus categories or does not seem to fit any of them. You can add or change Focus Cards as necessary while working through the exercise. Tape the Idea Card up under one of the

Focus Cards and read it aloud (translating any handwriting issues). As long as people can see the cards being mounted on the board, the Idea Cards will stimulate more ideas and more cards. Very quickly, usually within 15 minutes, the process generates more ideas than you can manage, and you shut it down.

At this point, we rank and discuss some of the better ideas. Ranking is done with the green dots or markers (good idea: "Like it") or red dots (bad idea*: "Don't like it"). Participants all approach the board with the collected Idea Cards mounted on it and each assigns three to five green dots and three to five red dots. After everyone has ranked the ideas, those with the most green dots are discussed further, and those with the most red dots are eliminated. You will still see some "group think" here, as people may vote for ideas that already have a number of green dots. In this case, the virtual version of storyboarding, done with computers, can eliminate the group think, as participants at a distance do not see which ideas are "liked" or "disliked" until totals are tallied.

Once ideas have been ranked, what happens next may be business dependent or related to the opportunity at hand. Often, the Idea Cards with the most green rankings can become Focus Cards for another pass through the process. The exercise can be repeated two or three times inside an hour or so, with the result being a collection of organized ideas leading to a process or a series of focused tasks. Names and resources are often assigned in the room as well.

Returning to our hotel example, under Customer Value, what do the customers really want in a budget hotel? Probably it is not five-star dining, spas, or a concierge service. At the end of the day (realistically and metaphorically), they want a good night's sleep in a safe and clean location. Idea Cards in this focus area that are on the mark may include

- Good sleep
- Good beds
- Quiet rooms

---

* Apparently in parenting classes today, new parents are now taught to say "Good idea," and "Not a good idea"; "Bad idea" is too negative for children.

- Convenient location
- Kid friendly
- Referrals to restaurants
- Loyalty program linked to the parent hotel chain

Under the Technology Focus Card, you may see

- Online reservation
- Automated check-in
- Wi-Fi Internet access (even in the budget category now)

Under the Construction Focus Card, you may find

- Low cost, but durable
- Sound insulation
- No pool, spa
- No restaurant
- Central location, near amenities

In reality, you would see dozens more ideas than these, but these are the relevant examples in our hotel case and normally score the most green dots. How do we give someone a good night's sleep? We provide a really good bed in a very quiet room. This seems contradictory in a budget hotel, so let us flip back to Chapter 2 and Lean for a minute. Lean focuses on value (what the customer really wants) and reduces or eliminates what the customer does not want or need. In this case, we will pay for the good beds and higher levels of sound insulation by reducing our spending in other areas. We will eliminate the pool, the restaurant, and the workout room. The lobby can be smaller but still very clean and well lit.

Will customers stay in our new hotel chain? It appears they would. What we have described is how Accor Hotel chain in Europe designed their Formule 1 brand for the budget segment[7]: smaller rooms, block construction with very durable furnishings, but great beds and well-insulated walls; automated check-in after hours to reduce staffing costs; and an otherwise unremarkable lobby. With such a design and concept, Formule 1 has grown to basically own the

Accor Formule 1	
Features we Lean out or Eliminate	Features we Enhance
• Restaurant	• Investment in quality beds and pillows
• Bar	• Sound insulation in walls, ceilings, and floors
• Spa or work-out area	
• Pool	
• Expansive lobby	
• Some after-hours staffing	

Figure 5.5 Lean Innovation and Accor Formule 1.

budget hotel segment in France, with market share of several times that of its competition (Figure 5.5).

Storyboarding is itself a process, but at a macro level it is a process for developing and implementing a strategy. It yields a visual map of associated ideas that evolve into a plan and the foundation for implementing or acting on that plan.

Our last approach in this chapter to generating ideas again relies on organizational and leadership culture within the firm. This is where we break some paradigms.

BREAKING PARADIGMS

My premise here returns to asking for help. In this case, work under the assumption that *every once in a while, you need to be able to ask for something exceptional from your people.* This is a core concept, and one of my three key responsibilities for leadership: We recognize opportunities, we avoid disasters, and we break paradigms. Here, ask for the unreasonable, explain why you need the outcome, provide the resources, and get out of the way. Sometimes, we amaze ourselves with what we can do. More important, your team will amaze you and themselves with what they are able to achieve. Here are some examples.

Every few years, the good folks at Habitat for Humanity do something incredible. They build a house from a clean piece of ground to a functional dwelling in under 4 hours. In 1999 in New Zealand, a crew of 140 built a four-bedroom home in 3 hours and 45 minutes. Habitat did it again in Alabama in 2002, this time in 3 hours and 30 minutes. Yes, the plumbing worked, and the lights turned on. On the first occasion in New Zealand, as the project finished, the Habitat team even arranged for a postal carrier to come by to deliver the family's first mail.[8]

In 1997, a group of British aerospace engineers built a car that could reach top speeds of 1,200 kilometers/hour. They are doing it again as we speak; this time the car could travel at 1,600 kilometers/hour, faster than the muzzle velocity of a .357 Magnum. It requires solid titanium wheels that would not fly apart at those speeds and has to be driven in the Bonneville salt flats of Utah. The only person willing (crazy enough?) to drive it is a former Royal Air Force test pilot.[9]

In 2006, the Stanford University football team kicked off the season in a brand new facility, a stadium that had been built in just 42 weeks, a timeline that included the demolition of the existing facility in the same location.* Typically, a project like this takes two or more years.

Months of planning go into activities like this. In the case of the Habitat properties, all parts of the house are assembled in modules simultaneously. A large crane is in place to put the roof on the walls as they are stood up. Electrical and plumbing installations are integrated into those modules where required as the walls and floors are fabricated. With the Stanford stadium project, several cranes were deployed, rather than one or two, enabling concurrent construction on different parts of the stadium. Even the grass sod was special, with 60 × 4 foot rolls brought in and rolled into place by tractor, vastly speeding up the process.

Why do we do things like this?

My focus on breaking organizational paradigms is a bit of a stretch for some groups as the payoffs for true stretch goals can seem obscure.

---

* Look up a video on this on YouTube: "Stanford football stadium construction." My preferred version shows time-lapsed photography to AC/DC background music.

I poll groups I work with on examples like those just mentioned and ask the "Why?" question. "Because we can," is a typical answer, which ultimately feels like saying we climbed Mt. Everest because it was there. I wonder what Sir Edmund Hillary would say to that? This is a challenging conversation, and I get some pregnant pauses and blank looks. That is not a reflection of the participants in the discussion; it is a statement of their organizations. We do not push enough.

We set stretch goals and targets and ask for something exceptional from our people to grow, to develop, and to learn things. We probably will not get it completely right, whatever "right" is, but we make progress in a forward direction.

In the late 1990s, my company received a call from Aston Martin, the British maker of premium automobiles. We had been talking to Aston for a while, trying to supply parts for one of their programs, but the company had always politely stated that it was happy with its existing supply base. Now, it was different: The company had a program for us. "Great," we said, "we'll be over next week, and we can talk about it." "Hold on," they responded, "this is a bit more complicated." It turns out that the existing supplier had walked away from the program, and Aston Martin was scrambling for a replacement. This program, in fact, was to launch in 13 months, and the vehicle was the latest version of the Aston Martin Vanquish, a machine that sells for about $500,000—each.

Our typical design and development cycle for a new program at that time was 24 to 30 months, depending on the complexity of the product. We were still a young company and building skills and capabilities in that side of our business. We talked after hanging up the phone with Aston: How would we cut our development time in half, including tooling up the parts and getting them through the quality approval process?

It did not take us long to decide. The opportunity to work on this level of vehicle with a company like Aston was too great. We took the program, with some provisos. We said we would be at the finish line when Aston needed us, but the route we took to get there would not be traditional; some of the typical milestones in an automotive launch would be sacrificed or modified. We developed a tentative timeline, to which Aston agreed. We set up virtual product and program reviews by video and teleconference, which was not really "done" at the time. Aston sent us a car (a prototype Vanquish) for testing parts and getting a feel for the type of vehicle we were now part of. This was a huge step made by Aston and what a great way to make sure our engineers were motivated, getting to drive and play with a vehicle that would otherwise be far out of reach.[*] More important, we were able to install, test, and trial parts in real conditions, seeing results much quicker than if we had to ship parts to Aston for review.

In the end, we hit the 13-month deadline, and the vehicle launched with our parts on it. There were a number of times through the development when we wondered what we were doing, but it worked out, with full credit to the team designing, developing, and tooling up the parts for manufacture. We went on to have a successful relationship with Aston Martin, with about $10 million a year in sales on the Vanquish, the DB9, and its new "entry-level" Aston Martin Vantage, priced at a very reasonable $120,000. They asked for the prototype Vanquish back when we launched the program, stating they had to have it crushed for tax purposes. We said that we would crush it for them (you can see what we were thinking), but they insisted. "But don't worry, we have another car on the way to you right now for the next program." I have to say that Aston was probably my favorite customer to work with.

Sales and customer benefits aside, substantial as they were, there were other achievements that came out of that first program with Aston. While we did not sign up for 13-month launch programs on a regular basis, we learned a great deal about the process by compressing our existing development cycle that time, and what we learned enabled the team to reduce our timing from 24 to 30 months to something closer to 20 when we needed to do so. That stretch target broke paradigms in our development process and enabled us to improve.

It is the same for the previous examples: Habitat for Humanity learns about modular construction by setting speed records on its properties. That saves Habitat time and costs on future buildings.

---

[*] Credit Jeff Potter, our sales manager, for asking Aston for the car.

The contractors that built the Stanford football stadium have a genuine artifact they can show perspective customers when they want something done quickly. "Yes, we can do that, and here is an example."

Breaking paradigms forces us to think about the problem differently and challenges people to develop new and innovative solutions. We learn. The key here is to agree on the goal, indicate why we are doing it, give the team the necessary resources, and get to it. Build in lots of follow-up and support, but keep that side of it as casual as possible. Additional bureaucracy will just bog down the process.

When was the last time you asked for something truly exceptional from your people (or yourself for that matter)? What was the last paradigm you broke?

In this chapter, we have focused on applying an innovative culture to generate ideas and solutions for challenges and problems faced by the organization. We need systems for collecting and dealing with ideas as they flow in from employees, customers, and suppliers. In other cases, we need to be able to force the idea process along. With the right environment, like your *i-space*, with storyboarding, or by breaking paradigms within the business, those concepts are again supported by a creative culture driven by the leadership of the organization.

Next, we look at what we do with those ideas, how they are refined and developed into a usable or commercially viable version of the original idea to the point of execution.

COOL IDEAS: TIM HORTON'S TIM CARD*

Most of you are familiar with the Tim Horton's coffee chain; it is hard to miss if you have been in Canada at all in the last 20 years, and its shops are now sprouting up in various northern states in the United States as well. Started by former NHL hockey player Tim Horton, the chain now has over 4,000 locations and millions of loyal Tim's fans who stop there multiple times per week, generating overall sales of $2.5 billion in 2010.

---

* http://www.timhortons.com.

A few years ago, Tim's launched the Tim Card, a prepaid card that you can use at Tim Horton's to pay for your coffee, donuts, lunch, or whatever you purchase. Gift certificates had been around for years, and the concept worked very well for Tim's. What better to buy your child's bus driver, soccer coach, or teacher than a prepaid Tim Card? Everyone likes coffee, right?

Every business in the world now seems to use gift cards, however, so what is the big deal here? Well, shortly after the launch, the smart folks at Tim Horton's started marketing the consumers' ability to "reload" their Tim Card with more money when it approached empty. Anyone with an Internet connection could now log on to the Tim Horton's site and put another $20 on the card (I know some people who reload it with $100 at a time).* The TV commercials were excellent, convincing us how easy and "cool" it was to reload the Tim Card. I sat down at my computer, about to reload one of the cards I had been given as a gift.

"Wait a minute," I thought. "I'm about to prepay for coffee." Not only are we paying $1.40 for a beverage that costs about 15 cents to make, but now I am going to send them $20 and tell them, basically, "I'll come and get the coffee some other time." So, I did not reload. I love the idea of a Tim Card as a gift or of most of the gift cards out there for other retailers. But, prepaying for coffee? Not me. Yet, the concept is working for Tim Horton's, and thousands of people reload on a regular basis, reaffirming their commitment to buy coffee at Tim's. People say how convenient it is, especially when they do not have any money. Um, really? Where do you carry the Tim Card? In your wallet, right next to your debit card—while this sounds like a "Who is on first?" discussion, Tim Horton's did not take plastic (debit or credit cards) of any type until recent years, operating as a strictly cash business.†

Statistics vary, but we know that the full value of gift cards, including Tim Cards, are rarely spent by consumers. So, we are in effect sending money to Tim Horton's ahead of time and not spending all of it when we get to the store.

---

* Starbucks has a similar program.
† I speculate in Appendix 1 that cash itself will disappear sooner rather than later, and ideas like the Tim Card and other micropayment cards will hasten the demise of cash.

Do not get me wrong; I am not criticizing Tim Horton's. I am suggesting that, as consumers, maybe we are not as smart as we think sometimes, which is great for Tim's and companies like it, but bad for us. But, how do we get ideas like that for our company?

COOL IDEAS: WALSHY STICK REPAIR[*]

Professional sports have seen their share of innovation, especially over the last 20 years as advertising and sponsorship investment has gone through the roof. Some of you may watch professional hockey, live or on television. One of the innovations that has taken off in recent years is the composite hockey stick, rendering virtually extinct the wooden variety some of us knew growing up. One of my favorite sticks as a kid was the Sherwood PMP 5030. Not that I was going to make it past minor league play, but hefting a new 5030 as a bantam player made me feel like a pro.

Enter technology: the vast majority of sticks now are made of carbon fiber, extruded and molded in manufacturing plants in China. Composite sticks are lighter with more consistent flex properties, colorful graphics, and a firmer "kick," supposedly giving the shooter the ability to make better, faster, or more accurate shots and ultimately more goals. This sounds great, right?

The challenge is the cost. Where the traditional wooden sticks were typically priced between $20 and $40, the new composite sticks now run from $40 for basic models at Costco to over $300 for pro-level sticks at a sporting goods store. Go back to the game you watch on TV; pay attention to how many of those $300 models get broken every game when the player is shooting or getting hacked by an opposing player. Between practices and games, pro teams now go through dozens of these sticks every week or hundreds throughout the season. This is not so bad for the pros, who through sponsorship get their sticks supplied free by companies like Bauer, Easton, and Warrior, but is very expensive for minor league teams and especially parents. While minor league and junior-level teams do not break as

---

[*] http://www.walshystickrepair.com.

many sticks as the pros, professionals are outnumbered by junior-level players almost 30:1 and by minor hockey players just in Canada by almost 900:1.* That is a lot of broken sticks and a lot of money.

Joey Walsh noticed that.

Walsh now operates a small business out of his shop near Belleville, Ontario, Canada, where he will repair broken composite sticks. Most of the repairs are in the shaft, where the stick breaks during the flex of a shot or from the impact of another stick hitting it. Walsh takes the two pieces and cuts off the damaged section to a smooth, squared-off edge. He then inserts a mesh plug, fills that section with fiberglass resin, clamps it, and lets it cure. The result is a stick that is an inch shorter, with a visible line in the shaft where it was repaired but is essentially fully operational. In fact, Walsh guarantees the stick will not break again in that location, the joint is so strong, and he has customers using the repaired sticks at the junior (semipro) level for the full season; one Wellington Duke player set a new scoring record in the 2011–2012 season using sticks repaired by Walsh.

The process does not make sense on an entry-level composite hockey stick, as Walsh sells the finished product for about $70, but customers are enthusiastic about getting $200 and $300 sticks for $70. Walsh also repairs broken or damaged blades.

Who are the customers? At the retail level, Walsh gets walk-in traffic from local representative and recreational teams for players aged between 12 and 60—players (or their parents) who will not go out and pay $300 for that stick, but give them the same stick for $70 with a few scratches on it, and they are in. I bought my son a Warrior brand stick at Walshy's that would have been $250 new at a traditional sporting goods store. Does it make a difference for him? Maybe not, but I would have paid about the same price for a cheaper stick anyway, and now Declan is carrying the same stick as a couple of his NHL idols. If he is happy, I am happy.

---

* Every minor sport player wants to be a professional and play in the big leagues; some of their parents buy into the hype as well. Turn the statistics around a bit, and the numbers provided indicate that about 1 child hockey player in 900 will make the NHL. (Source: http://www.hockeycanada.ca, 2012 annual report.)

Walsh is doing larger volume directly with junior, college, and higher-level rep teams, which ship him several dozen broken game sticks at a time. Walsh repairs them and ships them back, and the players use them for practices and games. He currently repairs around 50 sticks per week, with walk-in customers coming from a 100-mile radius around Belleville. Even better, southern Ontario is home to more than 40% of Canada's hockey market, and Walsh is the only operation like this in the neighborhood.

How do you come up with an idea like that? In this case, it was a combination of being around the sport and seeing the opportunity. Walsh and several cousins have been around competitive and junior hockey since they were old enough to walk. After finishing a sports management degree at Brock University in Ontario, Walsh traveled with Hockey Canada and the Vancouver Olympic Committee. In that environment, he saw his share of broken sticks, most often heading for the trash bin. At the Olympic tournament, he was introduced to a representative from Edgewater Industries in Spring Lake, Michigan, the company that developed the SRS (Shaft Repair System) stick repair technology. They talked, and Walsh brought the system to his shop in 2010.

Once again, this is an example of bringing an idea from another industry and solving a problem. The SRS technology itself with the carbon fiber mesh and fiberglass resin is employed for structural repairs to vehicles and aircraft, with the joint or repair location being stronger than the original material. Bringing the technology to sporting goods, with an endless supply of broken sticks and the largest market in the world—sounds like the shot is right on target.

NOTES

1. Drucker, P., *Innovation and Entrepreneurship*, Collins, New York, 1985.
2. Kim, W.C., and Mauborgne, R., "Blue oceans strategy," *Harvard Business Review*, p. 6, October 2004.
3. Alexander, A., "Whitening products brighten segment," September 12, 2011, http://www.drugstorenews.com.
4. Lafley, A.G., and Charan, R., *The Game Changer*, p. 99, Crown Business, New York, 2008.

5. Lafley and Charan, *Game Changer*, p. 142.
6. For more background on storyboarding and other great ideas, see *The Disney Way* by Bill Capodagli and Lynn Jackson (McGraw-Hill, New York, 2007).
7. Kim, W.C., and Mauborne, R., "Value innovation: the strategic logic of high growth," *Harvard Business Review*, July/August 2004, p. 6.
8. From the Habitat for Humanity Web site, http://www.habitat.org.
9. See http://www.bloodhoundssc.com or Satter, R.G., "Faster than a bullet," *Globe and Mail*, October 22, 2008.

6

Refining Ideas

It is what we know that often prevents us from learning.

Claude Bernard, French physiologist

When Reed Hastings launched Netflix in 1997, it looked a lot different than it does today. In a classic example of a great idea evolving from a dissatisfying experience, Hastings started the DVD movie-by-mail business after being charged over $40 in late fees when he discovered a delinquent copy of *Apollo 13* in his closet.[1]

At the time, the Internet was growing in popularity, as was online shopping and transactions over the Web. Connectivity speeds and bandwidth were increasing as well. Amazon and other virtual retailers were growing nicely, changing public perceptions about what could be done on the Internet. Congestion, traffic, and increasing fuel costs made staying home more appealing, supported by much improved home entertainment systems with exceptional video and audio capability.

When Netflix was born, Hastings and his team made some enhancements right away over the traditional movie rental model in the market dominated by Blockbuster: Netflix offered thousands of titles, compared to hundreds in your local Blockbuster. In the spirit of Lean, there were no physical storefronts, reducing the investment in real estate required by the company. Given Blockbuster's strategy of having a physical location within 15 minutes of 75% of the population, the investment required to compete on that level would have been extreme indeed. Netflix distribution centers for DVD inventories popped up around the United States very quickly to reduce shipping time to customers. DVDs arrived at your house with a prepaid envelope in the package; when you were done with the movie, you simply put it the prepaid envelope, dropped it in a mailbox, and forgot about it.

Still, there were issues, and customer adoption was not what Hastings had hoped. Challenges faced early on was a perception by customers who they were not being compensated for waiting for the DVD to arrive and some frustration related to the wait itself. In the Netflix model, customers select DVDs online, and those DVDs are then mailed to the customer. When we select a movie on a Wednesday, it could be Thursday or Friday (or later) before it arrives. Customers, however, were initially charged the same rental rate as they would pay when going to a Blockbuster location yet were forced to wait for the movie. Call this version of the company Netflix 1.0.

Netflix 2.0 (my words, not theirs) arrived not long after, once Hastings and his team evaluated customer feedback and the adoption rate of new subscribers. The big change with Netflix 2.0 was the unlimited subscription. For a flat fee of around $15, customers now could watch as many movies as they wished through the month. As well, viewers generally always had one or two movies from Netflix on hand, changing the "movie night" paradigm so that any night became movie night.

Netflix 2.0 also included a search algorithm on the Netflix Web site that helped customers find movies they would enjoy watching based on past selections and other movies they had in their queue. Similar in nature to the search process developed by Amazon, the algorithm added value for customers in a way the part-time retail help at a Blockbuster store never could.

The refinement of Netflix 1.0 to Netflix 2.0 is the primary reason the company is still here today (Figure 6.1). Many of their initial customers rented exactly one movie from Netflix before returning to their original movie habits. It was not until the improved version of Netflix came along that allowed unlimited rentals, no late fees,

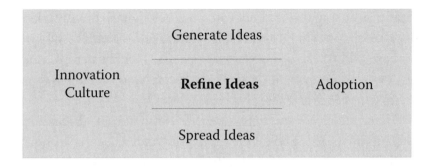

Figure 6.1 The innovation framework: refining ideas.

Netflix DVD Business	
Features we Lean out or Eliminate	Features we Enhance
• Physical store locations • Customer service reps in-store • Late Fees • Bad decision risk with movies customers pay for, but don't enjoy • Travel to / from rental store	• Broad movie selection (70,000 titles) • Selection algorithm to help find movies that suit our tastes • Movies on-hand (any night is *movie night*)

Figure 6.2 Lean Innovation at Netflix.

and "assistance" selecting movies that subscriptions really did take off. In fact, between 1999 and 2006, subscriber volumes increased by over 50% per year.* Netflix was not done refining its model either, as discussed later in this book.

When we compare Netflix to the incumbent Blockbuster in the video rental industry, we see that its fundamental approach to the business was very different from Day 1. Shunning storefronts and sales personnel, it focused instead on providing value for customers in the form of selection, assistance, and flexibility in their schedules (Figure 6.2). Blockbuster ignored the trend toward DVDs by mail

---

* Source: Company data.

initially, believing it would not catch on. When it eventually tried to offer that channel to customers, it was too late—Netflix's subscription base and track record were too strong. Blockbuster eventually filed for bankruptcy in both the United States and Canada as rentals and revenues declined sharply.

The story does not end here for either Netflix or our discussion of the company in this book. One innovation and a successful startup does not make a company, despite Netflix having over $50 million in the bank in 2007. Technology and consumer viewing habits are changing rapidly, so we circle back to Netflix in Chapter 8 to discuss what is next for Hastings and the team with video on demand. Their durability in the market place is still to be determined. They have, at least temporarily, exploited an opportunity, but as the online market evolves, longevity is far from ensured.

The most significant reason an innovation does not stick in the market is a failure to identify the appropriate target market for the idea. Part of the appeal of innovation is the ability of the idea to attract new customers to our market. Our challenge is understanding who those customers will be as chances are most existing customers will be satisfied with the current offering available to them in the market. One could argue that Hasting's 1.0 version of Netflix targeted the wrong customer, the movie night "event" customer who wanted the movie now. That version of Netflix needed to be refined to seek the appropriate customers and market.

In his book, *The Innovator's Dilemma*, Clayton Christensen described the fundamental concept of disruptive innovation[2]; according to this, players in existing markets failed to see the threat of new entrants, working under the reasonable theory that their customers would be happy with what they were currently receiving. In most cases, the incumbents were right: Their existing customers were satisfied and less interested in significant changes to the product or service. Makers of minicomputers wanted the eight-inch disk drives to be faster and less expensive. If there were a smaller disk drive (5¼-inch) that runs slower than the existing drives with less storage capacity? They were not interested.

It turns out it was not the minicomputer market that the 5¼-inch drives appealed to; it was the quickly developing home *microcomputer* market, in which size was given a premium over speed. These were brand new customers and products that the eight-inch disk drive people had not considered, a market that quickly outpaced the minicomputer market in terms of volume and technology growth. The manufacturers of 8-inch drives did not react in time and quietly disappeared.

In the Netflix case, Hasting's model for Netflix was the disruptive innovation, pursuing new DVD customers rather than existing VHS customers. VHS tapes would not have worked in the Netflix model; shipping costs would have been prohibitive, warehouse space requirements would have been three times as large for the same number of titles, and the tapes themselves would be subject to more damage in the mail and by consumers at home. While Blockbuster continued to focus on VHS and eased into DVDs, Netflix built an entirely new model around the small, durable disks. Blockbuster ignored this model until it was too late to effectively react.

Refining our ideas involves several steps, as noted in Figure 6.3. Interestingly, the refining phase, like the overall innovation framework, does not need to involve all steps or necessarily proceed in order; we can also thin slice here. What is most important is that we push hard to see what is wrong with our idea before launching significant investment.

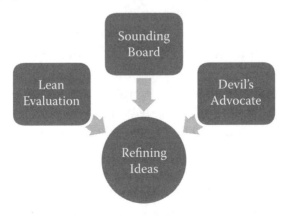

Figure 6.3 Refining ideas.

Before committing to his DVD-by-mail business, Hastings packaged up a couple dozen CDs and mailed them from different locations in different packaging to himself, testing the durability of the media when transported through the post. CDs and DVDs are made of polycarbonate, coated with aluminum and a protective barrier. It is uncommon for one of the disks actually to break in transit, but scratching can occur, which essentially destroys the movie. Through this low-cost evaluation process, Hastings developed several packaging options and ultimately determined that the shipping and transportation part of his business model would work fine.

LEAN EVALUATION

Observation is a passive science; Experimentation is an active science.

Claude Bernard

People have difficulty sometimes understanding the appeal or application of a new concept. When we ask someone what they think of an idea, we struggle to explain it in a manner that provides sufficient context, value, and perspective. For many of us, this is a limitation in our grasp of language or perhaps failing to turn on the charisma and really *sell* the idea. What we need in many cases is something physical to make the concept real: a model, prototype, drawing, process flow diagram. The best examples are models that people can see, touch, taste, and experience with their senses.

At the same time, however, we do not know yet if we have something the market wants, so investing too much initially in the development of scale models and prototypes would not make good business sense. We need some way of evaluating concepts on the cheap, like Hastings did in mailing CDs to himself.

Discussed next are some examples.

Joe Rohde was pitching the idea for a new theme park to Disney chief executive officer (CEO) Michael Eisner. The concept involved creating an environment where guests to Disney interacted much more intimately with wild animals in something designed to be much closer to their original habitats. Rides, attractions, and the park itself would be designed around the animals. Eisner was not convinced. He just did not see the appeal of wild animals; the experience was commonplace now in the zoos found in most major cities. Rohde had anticipated Eisner's reluctance and opened the door to the conference room. In walked a petite young lady holding a leash, on the end of which was a 300-pound Bengal tiger. She walked the tiger around the room, then stopped the big cat and stood quietly in the corner of the room. Eisner quickly saw the appeal of wild animals, and in 1998 Rohde got the approval and funding for what became Disney's Animal Kingdom.[3]

When he was 15 years old, Michael Dell bought an Apple computer. Dell, being a curious sort, took the computer apart to see how it worked. Imagine the expression on his parents' faces when they saw the $3,000 computer lying in pieces on Dell's bed. No worries: he quickly reassembled the computer, and everything worked fine. That process, however, helped the young Dell understand that home computers were really a series of modules and components that could be replaced easily. His curiosity and aptitude led him to upgrade various components in the Apple II computer with components he purchased from mail order catalogues (the Internet was not at the home shopping stage in 1980).

Later, in college, he began assembling computers for friends and contacts, again buying the components directly from manufacturers and bypassing traditional retailers, middlemen, and their related markups. Customers of Dell received very good machines at a lower cost than traditional retail, and they could design a "custom" computer à la carte. Dell realized he was onto something and dropped out of college to focus full time on his business.[4] In 1984, his first full year in business, Dell did over $6 million in sales and by 2001 had overtaken Compaq as the world's largest computer maker.

In 1980, Lee Iacocca wanted Chrysler to look at making a convertible. No North American car company had made a convertible since 1976, when Ford dropped that line of Mustang. Iacocca asked his marketing people to get a sense of the business potential and his engineering team to develop a plan for a prototype. The marketing folks came back with an estimate of just 3,000 cars, hardly enough to justify the capital and tooling investment in the vehicle.[5] Engineering indicated it would take nine months to create the prototype for evaluation. Frustrated with both responses, Iacocca said, "You don't understand. Take a car, cut the roof off and let me look at it."[6] A month later, the prototype arrived from the body shop. Iacocca drove it around Detroit and Florida himself and proceeded with the car based on the favorable responses he received when people saw it.

The Chrysler Town and Country convertible was launched in 1983, and while volumes were never huge, 24,000 of the cars were sold (eight times the marketing estimate) and were likely responsible for reigniting North American drivers passion for convertibles. Today, most car companies offer a convertible.

What do these examples have in common? They all involved low-cost evaluation of an idea, and the evaluation involved some type of model, test, or experiment that made the concept *real* for the audience. That evaluation better enables us to place a value on and understand the concept. That understanding is crucial in determining the best way to spread and launch the idea, as we will see in the next chapter.

The second part of that equation relates back to the number of experiments we can run. Trying multiple versions of an idea generates more usable data: More generations result in more failures but, more importantly, better revision to the overall concept. The final version can evolve with something from several of the trials built into it. Cut the cost of your trials and experiments and run as many different angles as you can.

Jeff Hawkins, founder of Palm and Handspring and creator of the Palm Pilot, initially carried a model of the device about the size of a deck of cards made out of balsa wood in his shirt pocket, giving him a sense of what his customers would go through and how they would interact with the device. He built the early model himself in his garage, drilling a hole in the wood for the "stylus" (made out of a chopstick) and gluing on a graphic printed on his computer to simulate the touch screen.[7] He would bring out the mock-up in meetings and "write" on the screen (picture that conference room: "What's

Jeff doing?"). This experimentation led him to understand his device would be competing with a pen and paper, not other computing devices, which simplified his focus and kept him from building too many bells and whistles into the first Palm handheld PDAs (personal digital assistants).[8] As well, the model itself was a big part of changing the company strategy to that of a product-based company.

THE SOUNDING BOARD

Advice is seldom welcome; and those who want it the most always like it the least.

Phillip Stranhope, Fourth Earl of Chesterfield

You asked for my opinion. If you're not going to follow it, why did you ask?

Don Smith, Black & Decker director of new products, about 1980

Innovation is a social process. That perception we have of the creative genius banging away in a garage really will not typically generate a commercialized idea. At best, he or she will come up with a 1.0 concept with limited market appeal.

In his book, *The Myths of Innovation*, Scott Berkun discussed the concept of the "lone innovator" stuck in a wardrobe of existing ideas.[9] Think about that: Our ability to generate new, commercially viable ideas by ourselves is extremely limited. We "get" an idea through input from other parties, media, people watching in the subway, or taking a new route home from work. Without that outside input, we are restricted by our existing knowledge, beliefs, paradigms, and biases. We need to remove the blinders to see beyond those biases to effectively refine the idea.

One of my biases, for example, is that I do not think carrot cake should really be called a cake. After all, it is made out of carrots, not the stuff we know world-class bakers would put in their cakes. French bakers, you can imagine, would express shock and outrage at the idea of any such vegetable being in one of their cakes. I can kind of get my head around the idea of a carrot muffin—a healthier muffin sounds like a decent way to start the day—but cakes are dessert, and a healthy dessert is an oxymoron and not the way to wrap up a nice meal. So, when friends or relatives serve carrot cake for dessert or, *gasp*, a celebration, my bias prevents me from enjoying it. I blame marketing people for somehow convincing people that carrot cake is actually a cake. I am not sure when or how it happened, but I am quite convinced some rogue baker got the right public relations firm, and here we are. A good ad person can sell anything.

We all have biases, habits, beliefs, and prejudices like this. You have superstitions: you always put one shoe on first or fold your pants a certain way; you have a favorite parking space at work, or you habitually order the grandé caramel latte at Starbucks; you have a customary seat at the conference room table in the Friday management meeting. Most of us are creatures of habit and consistent in our basic beliefs, and those patterns keep us inside the box. Our ability to see, as we saw in the awareness test video in Chapter 2, is shaped by those beliefs, biases, and paradigms. Breaking paradigms is an active process we can apply, as discussed in Chapter 5. Fresh thinking, ideas, and creativity require influence outside our internal operating framework, and refining those ideas is an especially social process.

We think of a sounding board as someone we bounce ideas off to get the person's feedback or input. Sounding boards, when applied effectively, can take on formal and informal roles within our innovation system. Think of food critics evaluating our restaurant or travelers posting on Trip Advisor about our hotel property. These people provide either an "expert" or informed opinion on our service, allowing us to shape and fine-tune our offering to resolve issues or emphasize the things we are doing well.

Through social media-like user groups, blogs, LinkedIn, and Facebook, we now have access to sounding boards that are orders of magnitude greater than anything we are familiar with as company leadership. With that access, however, comes significant responsibility. When the reviews are positive, life is good—people "like" us. When something negative is posted, we had better be paying attention. Ask United Airlines about its new social media and customer service response plan after the "United Breaks Guitars" video exploded on YouTube. Dave Carroll's video, depicting harsh treatment of his guitar and nonresponsive customer service from United, quickly became a sensation (or "went viral" in social media parlance), having been seen by over 11 million viewers at the time of this writing. Interestingly, by the time United decided to make good with Mr. Carroll, he was a folk hero, musician, and keynote speaker on effective customer service as a result of the experience. It is a different world out there now.

Managing our social media strategy is usually an innovation tactic for refining and improving existing company offerings, but creative firms such as Apple are getting out ahead of the curve as well. Somehow early versions of the iPhone 4 and 4S were "lost" in San Francisco bars, where at least one ended up in the hands of a tech blogger, who was able to write about it before the company released it in the fall of 2010. While the engineer who forgot his prototype at a bar in California was apparently reprimanded, it is believed that the company intentionally got a few of the phones out there ahead of the launch to start building Web and media hype.[10]

More often, sounding boards are internal or development tactics for ideas just out of the germination phase or perhaps at the stage of testing and prototyping. How should this work? Recognize first that people generally do not like new ideas. Berkun spent some time on this concept as well in his *Myths* book. Think about the lukewarm responses and facial expressions you have seen when bouncing something by a colleague or supervisor: the brows wrinkle, the eyes squint, the lips purse; the shoulders hunch up a bit; sometimes the hands fold in a contemplative manner in front of them. Then, "That's a good idea, but … ," and it is canned.

While we talked about issues with communication in selling our idea, there are also problems here with our timing and the environment. We have talked about our ongoing drive for efficiency in most businesses. People are busy doing what they do. Even in an atmosphere with an open door policy, the ground rules around that open-door invitation is that we keep the visit to less than 5 minutes, we do not ask any really tough questions, and suggestions or ideas are frowned on.

("Who do you think you are trying to make me think?! I'm busy!") As Berkun said, do not worry about someone stealing your idea. For it to be accepted, you will have to ram it down their throats.

So, in the interest of making the idea more palatable to the people acting as our sounding boards, we need to box out some time for them to hear it. Request a meeting rather than spring it on the person and tell the person you have some thoughts on a problem the firm is facing, which leads us to the next consideration we discuss. It really does not matter if we are in leadership or the trenches. Give the recipient the benefit of knowing the context of your discussion ahead of time, and the idea will be more warmly received.

What problem are we solving? Putting the right sounding board together is a factor of where the problem is or what opportunity the idea may present. The idea connects to something, however abstract it may seem at this time. Does it simplify the customer interface? Does it eliminate a step in an online transaction? Does it solve something customers have highlighted as an issue to us, or will it reduce errors below the line of visibility to the customer? Once we identify the problem we are solving, we can decide who needs to be in the room. If the person on the receiving end of the idea pitch owns the problem, the person will be much more receptive to hearing the idea.

Beyond who *needs* to be present is who *should* be present. It may sound like we are playing with words, but this is about getting fresh perspectives, as discussed previously. In this case, a cross-functional approach with people not connected to the problem or even the business unit is beneficial.

The body of customers has several roles in the refinement process for new ideas. The idea may benefit them, but consider if it is still clunky to use or apply. Also, as an idea is refined, it involves different *types* of customers at different phases of its evolution. Figure 6.4 depicts a simple product life cycle, with four phases of customer adoption for a new product[*]: early adopters, early majority, majority, and late majority.

---

[*] This could also be a service life cycle, representing the different stages of uptake of a new service. This version is adapted from the original developed by economist Raymond Vernon in 1966 to combine the maturity and saturation phases.

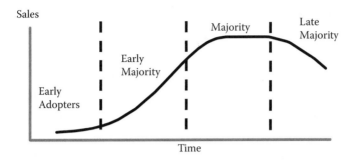

Figure 6.4 The product life cycle.

What do our customers *look like* in these phases? How do they behave, and what motivates them? It surprises some people to learn that each phase has customers who are unique to that part of the cycle. Rare is the case when a customer sticks with a product or service from its inception to its death.

Think about the latest tech gadget to come out, maybe a new music device. The product has just been launched, so there are likely still a few bugs to work out. It works differently from anything we have seen so far in the marketplace. Assuming it does what it is designed to do and is marketed appropriately, it will attract customers. This first group of users are the early adopters. You know people like them. They are audiophiles, passionate about music, and are excited by new technology. Maybe they are musicians or appreciate different genres of music, but they probably know more about the music and related technology than anyone you know. They try new products and devices all the time. Some products are "crap," in their words, but others really get their attention, and they talk on and on about them. They get *geeked up* about products like this. They know there will be issues with the 1.0 version, but they do not mind working through those problems. They are probably part of user groups[*] and may even provide feedback to the organization that launched the product to help make it better.

The early adopters are crucial to the refinement of new products and services. That first group of customers provides modest

---

[*] User groups are often unofficial or nonsanctioned groups of loyal and enthusiastic customers.

production volumes to the company to get their production or service processes sorted out and, when tapped accordingly, help tune the product from a 1.0 to a 2.0 version. Without refining the commercialized version of the idea, it is doomed to die an expensive death at the hands of demanding customers and agile competitors. A big part of that need for refinement is due to the nature of the next category of customers.

Early majority customers have one thing in common with the early adopters: They like to be the first on their block to have something. For them, it is less about the pleasure of figuring out a new toy than about prestige and visibility. Therefore, the gadget has to work reliably and as expected. All the bugs have to have been worked out of the 1.0 version, and some enhancements have to have been made that really make it appealing. The upside for us as an organization is that the early majority brings the 2.0 version of our product more sales volume, and we actually start to see financial returns from the idea. As the product is refined further and the volumes continue to increase, we may see the price come down somewhat, and the product becomes more of a value purchase.

At this stage, we see the majority adopt the product, and we can say that the innovation in that state is mature. It is no longer "new." It is unlikely that any early adopters are still on board; they have probably moved on to the next big thing. Early majority individuals are considering the replacement of the device with the next generation and maybe selling their current model on craigslist or Kijiji.

The final phase of customers are the late majority, or the laggards. Rarely part of a marketing strategy, this group does not purchase a new product or service until forced to do so, as in the old version of what they want is no longer available or they need to adopt the technology to stay in the game. It will not be very long before we will not be able to buy CDs in stores; people will have to buy digital copies through, say, iTunes and load the music on their iPod or other player if they want to listen to new music.

The next question is, where do we make money on this curve? Given the struggles in launching a new product—research and development (R&D) costs, its associated scrap, inventory, reduced line rates as we ramp up, lower initial sales volumes, and the marketing and advertising costs associated with priming customers to look at the product—the best we can hope for in the early adoption phase is to break even. More often, by the time development costs are amortized in, we lose money for some time. Once the volumes of the early majority hit, however, things can start to look good. We expect that margins are highest in this phase. Really, we need to be making money in the early majority and majority stages of a new product or service, and without the evolution of the innovation to the 2.0 version, that does not happen. We need to be thinking about what is coming next while we enjoy the benefits of that last innovation.

Most companies gravitate toward one position on the product or service life cycle for their industry and get very good at managing those cycles. Their position on the curve becomes part of their brand and image, and customers implicitly recognize the company's premium or value associated with that position. Firms such as Audi and Lexus, for example, live primarily in the early majority stage, working with lower sales volumes, but charging a premium for the improved technology, performance, and comfort associated with their brands.

One of the key issues we face here is the disconnect between the early adopters and the early majority. Refining ideas is the bridge between those very different groups of customers that enables the idea to have some form of longevity. The transition between early majority and majority categories is less severe; here, we are really looking at an increase in value, delivered by adding features, reducing cost, or making the service more accessible.

THE DEVIL'S ADVOCATE

We have discussed a number of tactics for examining ideas and reviewing them as a team with the expectation that the idea would evolve and improve to the point of something commercially acceptable. What if the idea itself does not deserve investment by the organization? How is that determined? How do we effectively challenge new ideas?

Part of the review process discussed about Figure 5.3, idea review, involves consideration at Screen 1 of whether we *should* pursue an idea. The key hurdle is how well the idea connects to and supports the current strategy and vision of the organization. Some of the same challenges we discussed concerning brainstorming apply here as well. Inside a Screen 1 meeting, unless those in the group are confident that they are expected to challenge each other, the presence of *groupthink* is quite likely. An idea is presented, discussed, but never really challenged. There is lots of head nodding and polite questions, but generally the motion is carried. Sometimes, it is the fact that the team is so busy, the fear of a long, drawn-out discussion prevents people from speaking up. In other cases, participants are too sensitive to the feelings in the room to challenge an idea. While we may scoff at the idea of a culture like that existing in our boardroom, we have all been in that very meeting.

Alfred P. Sloan, long-time chairman and CEO of General Motors, was famous for pushing back on his leadership team in that very situation. In one often-cited quotation, he said, "If we are all in agreement on the decision?" Heads nod around the table. "Then I propose we postpone further discussion of this matter until our next meeting to give ourselves time to develop disagreement and perhaps gain some understanding of what the decision is all about."[11]

Some organizations have taken the step of formalizing this process inside their strategy reviews, adopting a role used in the canonization process by the Catholic Church for centuries before it was abolished by Pope John Paul II in 1983. This role was called the promoter of the faith or, less formally, the devil's advocate.* The devil's advocate, a senior cardinal and expert in canon law, would be charged with researching and presenting a case why an individual should not be canonized or appointed a saint by the Church. They look for flaws in the person's character or history, challenge miracles attributed to that person, and essentially argue against the proposed sainthood. The last thing the Church wanted was to be embarrassed

---

* My first exposure to the concept of a devil's advocate was in religion class at the Catholic high school I attended in 1981. At the time, being able to apply the concept in business was the last thing on my mind.

by any flaws surfacing after an individual was canonized, so it built in this hurdle process.*

Merriam-Webster calls the devil's advocate the "Roman Catholic official whose duty (it) is to examine critically the evidence on which a demand for beatification or canonization rests," and further, "a person who champions the less accepted cause for the sake of argument."[12]

Paul Carroll and Chunka Mui proposed the use of the devil's advocate as a formal role inside leadership chambers[13] to argue the no side and keep the organization from doing something that might lead to catastrophe or, at best, deviate from the vision of the company. I use the devil's advocate role here to refine ideas as much as question their validity. Yes, some ideas die a swift death through this discussion, which is absolutely appropriate and part of the process, but just as many are fine-tuned, refined, and improved into better versions of themselves.

Carroll and Mui acknowledged, however, the challenges faced by that devil's advocate. When the "no" side wins, someone else loses. People at this level in the company have long memories and big egos, so filling the role would be an ongoing challenge, and the process would fail without some guidelines. When used as a tool for refinement, both sides win as the idea is improved. The idea champion and the challenger both contributed to its success.

How would it work in your organization? For me, this is a role that would have to rotate among members of the group. Taking on the role for a project, and doing it seriously, would be an enlightening experience that would shape our perspective on future projects. If we can build the customer's needs into the dialogue, even better. Maybe the devil's advocate represents the customer or even the competitors. Sometimes, that does not even need to be a real person. One company I know bought a crash test dummy on eBay, put "him" in a suit, and parked him in the corner of the main conference room. They named the dummy Dave (making no intended connection between the name Dave and dummies everywhere). Dave did not say

---

* Since the role was abolished in 1983, almost 500 people have been canonized by the church, five times the number that were recognized for sainthood through the rest of the 20th century. Many of these, however, were canonized en masse; groups of people were recognized for extraordinary sacrifices in support of the church. (Source: http://www.vatican.va.)

much, but when the team needed to get the customer's perspective on something, Dave was wheeled up to the table and symbolically represented the voice of the customer. It seemed to work for them.

In other cases, the devil's advocate role is a process instead of a person. In the proposal of the idea, project, or strategy, part of the risk management process is to highlight what can go wrong with the idea and then develop countermeasures to that risk. In the product engineering world, there is a process called failure mode and effects analysis or FMEA (engineers like to give things acronyms; three-letter acronyms or TLAs are preferred). A FMEA is basically a table with a list of what can potentially go wrong and a numerical ranking or representation of how bad it can get. Scores are achieved by multiplying the severity of the problem by the likelihood that it could happen and by the likelihood we can catch the problem before the customer sees it. The product of those three numbers is ranked against all the other risks, and then the team can figure out how to deal with the worst possible offenders.

Do not underestimate the scope of this process; while extremely powerful when done right, it is also very tedious. The challenge is getting people to commit to the time associated with running a FMEA event. It can often take four hours to run through the first pass, with further work and meetings involved in getting tentative solutions to the high-risk issues. So, lots of work is needed, but it is a valuable tool in the right environment.*

As projects become more strategic and "leading edge," it can be more difficult to get the FMEA review team to predict the risks of the projects. The newness of the idea itself creates a disconnect with the possible risks in the development of the idea; essentially, the team struggles to think of what can go wrong. In this case, it is important to allow sufficient time in the development process for those issues to arise and be resolved.

The last area of focus in this section is the makeup or chemistry of the executive team. Our natural inclination when putting a group

---

* This process got some traction in our organization in the DN101 program discussed previously. Several of the production issues we ran into had been highlighted in the FMEA process weeks earlier.

like this together is to surround ourselves with like-minded people. Whether it is the leadership team or a project group, we need to resist that urge. Having someone who pushes back from time to time, gently or otherwise, can help us avoid making some pretty large mistakes. Maybe this person is pessimistic by nature, perhaps grouchy, or the person just thinks a bit differently from the rest of us (more on this person in Chapter 8). Either way, rather than being appointed a devil's advocate, the person's personality puts the person in that position on a daily basis. The person pushes back, challenges, and forces us to think things through. A new member on the team can have the same effect. Someone who has recently joined the group will not have the same biases and belief system burned in yet, so this fresh perspective can allow the person to ask questions the team has not thought of yet.

At Pixar, the review team is referred to as the Brain Trust.[14] Inside a meeting to review a movie pitch, there is no room for egos and no expectation to be polite. The devil's advocate is, in essence, everyone. All members of the Brain Trust are expected to challenge, support, laugh, cajole, and engage, driving a fast but intense understanding by the team of whether they have a winning concept or not. That input allows the director of the proposed movie to shape its direction, even if it means killing the project altogether.

The devil's advocate embodies the social aspect of innovation and is part of the refinement process for ideas by helping us see the downside in the idea. That perspective ensures the team is not going into an initiative with the proverbial rose-colored glasses on, anticipating a smooth and trouble-free launch leading to global domination. When we look at the risks or trouble spots associated with the idea, we start working around them, and the idea itself is refined to a stronger and more robust version of itself.

IDEA FAILURE

Think about our previous CVS Pharmacy example. Once the team has developed a process for filling prescriptions it thinks will work, how would the team go about testing it? If I was on that team, I would suggest a combination of the refinement tactics we have discussed.

My low-cost evaluation would be to trial the new process at several test stores. I would select stores from both high-volume urban locations and lower-traffic spots in more rural settings. I would also include stores from different parts of the country. The market test would involve perhaps only a few stores but would evolve in waves. Run a trial in one store to verify we are not risking patient safety in the dispensing process and make any necessary changes. Run the next version in three to five locations and refine as necessary. Repeat the process again with a larger sampling, but the same group of stores would participate in the trials to minimize the variables of the experimentation.

Our sounding board would be the employees (pharmacists and technicians) and customers associated with the trials. We would have people from customer care and marketing from CVS headquarters talking to employees and customers going through the process. In other cases, they would just watch the process, keeping track of the time spent in line, customer and employee mood, and the overall flow through the area. What do people like? What would they change? Talk to doctors and representatives from the drug companies: What issues do they see in the existing and proposed processes?

Our devil's advocate process would be done two ways, first by putting a pharmacist or two on our planning team (CVS did this). The pharmacist present offers a perspective from the customer, is familiar with the process within the store, and will quickly highlight challenges or issues with our plan we may not have considered otherwise. As well, that pharmacist can go back and talk to peers at other CVS stores and help sell the plan. *Yes, I was part of the process for this. It really looks like something that will make our lives easier.* The pharmacist's involvement facilitates the roll out and acceptances by other pharmacists or users.

Second, we send some of our team members out to get prescriptions filled by our competitors, say Walgreen's or Wal-Mart. Getting a sense of what is happening inside the other stores will give us critical feedback with what we are planning at CVS.

I reiterate one point we touched on previously, however, regarding benchmarking. From an innovation perspective, we do not benchmark within our industry for "best practices." I see little benefit in trying to make our organization like others in our business. CVS benchmarks to verify customers have the same problems at other pharmacies, to make sure our great new process is not already being done by a competitor, and to see other possible "watch outs" regarding the script process overall. That makes sense to me and is easily done. Benchmarking for the purposes of generating ideas in innovation is done outside our industry and business model.

One of the benefits of the refinement process we have not discussed is the concept of selling the idea internally. As we run more trials and get input from the dozens of employees involved, they are getting on board with the change. Managing this change to their existing process is essential and one of the key concepts we discuss in the next chapter. Their engagement here drives their support and enthusiasm.

An idea needs to be refined, tuned, and in some cases provoked into failure early in the spirit of evolving into a better version of itself. Some ideas will evolve, and others will die in refinement. It is okay to fail. If it is a priority for the organization to drive creativity and new ideas, we need to accept that there is inherent uncertainty associated with that process. We resolve the uncertainty with a robust trial-and-evaluation process. The more things we try, the more will fail, but with each failure we hone in on what we believe is the future version of that idea.

Lean (Chapter 2) keeps us from pursuing the wrong strategy for too long. The idea of unlimited resources allows people to pursue the wrong strategy for a long time, when the probability that we will get it right the first time is extremely low.[15] Maintaining a focus on value will bring the experimentation back to what matters most, and that is what the customer wants.

Some revisions are simple, like Wal-Mart suggesting to Proctor and Gamble (P&G) that their Swiffer dust sweeper should be mounted on a stick.[16] Others drive platform-level enhancements to existing products already in the portfolio. Still with P&G, Clorox disinfectant wipes and Armor All wipes were born of the concept of baby wipes.[17] The refine process can correct issues in the delivery process, as with CVS, or prevent the launch of something that should have stayed on the drawing board, like the Iridium satellite phone project from Motorola, discussed further in the next section.

In all cases, revision is a social process, involving team members, employees, customers, and sometimes suppliers or competitors. The 1.0 version of our idea has a place: to help the organization get to a 2.0 version that will really appeal to the market. The 1.0 version should be tested, challenged, reviewed, bent, broken, tasted, and turned, but if it gets launched, it is a limited release to capture attention and input from early adopters. It is not a bad idea, but we need to make it better. Version 2.0 should be close on 1.0's heels.

Refinement not only improves on the idea but also prepares our organization for the idea itself, training employees how to deal with the idea and its related processes and warming the team up to the change in the company's identity. It reinforces company culture, a culture of innovation where we look after our current customers, but we are always thinking about who the next customers are and what they look like. Refinement can also prepare those customers for the idea. They have heard about the preliminary version, maybe in a tech blog or company press release or through other users. We use the testing and validation process to build momentum in the marketplace, getting it ready for the spread, as we discuss in the next chapter.

MOTOROLA IRIDIUM SATELLITE PHONE SYSTEM

The Motorola Iridium satellite phone seemed like a good idea at the time.

In MBA and executive seminars on innovation and project execution, I use the term *hideous project failure* to describe some of the more significantly questionable projects in society's collective portfolio. One of the more popular cases, and perhaps one of the biggest and widely reported project failures of all time, Motorola's Iridium satellite phone system disaster could have been avoided with some fundamental changes to the refinement process within their development skunk works.* Initially conceived by Motorola engineers in the late 1980s, really in the dawn of cellular communications, the plan for Iridium was to blanket the globe with a network of 70 satellites that would enable worldwide communications for all of us. At the time, cell phone coverage was spotty, roaming was difficult and expensive, and cooperation among networks was limited, so true mobility was a justifiable pursuit.

When the engineers presented the idea to Motorola leadership, enthusiasm filled the room. Checks were written, teams were committed, and the future state of global communications was envisioned. As early as 1990, however, Motorola engineers reported to leadership that there were several significant limitations to the system. Handsets were anticipated to cost $3,000 each, out of reach of the majority of consumers. Airtime would be very expensive, something like $6 per minute.[18] Most significantly, the cost of the satellites necessary for such a system was anticipated to be in the billions of dollars.[19] As well, to get broadcast approval, Motorola would have to get licensing from the telecommunications bodies of the 170 countries where Iridium would be functional.[20]

Motorola ran the numbers associated with these estimates and realized it would need over 1 million subscribers to make the project work.[21] Even with that information, leadership approved the project's next phase, and millions of lines of code to manage the satellite communications were written. Service was eventually launched in 1998, but Motorola achieved barely 50,000 subscribers.

Wayne Gretzky, arguably the greatest hockey player to ever play the game, used to say that he would never skate to where the puck is but to where it was going. In the dozen years it took Motorola to launch Iridium, the puck moved. While they were developing the system, GSM and multiband cell phones came on the market.

---

* *Skunk works* is a term used to describe a lab or innovation environment where the approach to solving a problem is different from what the firm traditionally uses. Coined near the end of World War II, the skunk works was the area where a new jet was developed and built in 143 days to exceed the capabilities of German jets at the time. The term is now trademarked by Lockheed Martin Advanced Development. (Source: http://www.opusvl.com.)

Cell phone companies realized their customers traveled and began offering cooperation agreements between carriers. More cell towers were erected and the handset quality improved, with more features and less size and cost. In the end, most of us did not really need a global satellite phone system.

Shortly after launch in 1999, Iridium filed for Chapter 11 bankruptcy protection, unable to pay the debts associated with its mammoth investment. Liquidators eventually bought the satellites and assets for $20 million, and the new Iridium currently boasts roughly 250,000 subscribers, including the U.S. military and various corporations operating in remote points of the world.

There are a number of lessons that come out of a case like Iridium. Executive hubris is obviously near the top of the list. We cannot let our beliefs cloud rational judgment. In the innovation model we are applying here, there really was no challenge presented against the project at any time during its development. Even in the face of some of the estimated costs, leadership said, "Carry on!" Where was even one confident executive, challenging the level of investment in this project before proceeding?

Hindsight being what it is, we would suggest a number of steps in refining Motorola's innovation of the Iridium system. Build some model handsets. The first generation of these phones were clunkers. Perhaps getting some models in the hands of leadership may have slowed things a bit. "This is heavy as a brick, and it doesn't fit in my pocket!"

Launch one satellite, if we get that far, over the Rocky Mountains or jungles of Costa Rica. Send operators out to test how the devices work in challenging environments. We would see then that the handsets have to be line of sight to the satellite. They will not work in caves, under large trees, or more practically, inside a building or a car. "Hmm. This certainly has some operator restrictions. 'Can you hear me now?'"

Assess what our competitors, the traditional cell companies, are doing at the time. We would have seen the evolution of the cell phone and, it is hoped, reassessed the likelihood of achieving a million subscribers. "Who is our customer, and what do they want? The puck has moved; what does that do to our business plan?"

Perhaps refining our project leads to a dozen satellites, rather than 70. Position the satellites over places like South America and Africa for mining operations, adventurers, and extreme travelers or humanitarian aid organizations. Spend some of the satellite investment we have eliminated on improving the handsets, making them smaller and lighter. Maybe in that structure, call it Phase 1, the launch of Iridium would have succeeded, possibly leading to the next generation of the system.

Carroll and Mui cited the Motorola Iridium as one of the most significant of their billion dollar lessons, a very apt description. With some leadership reflection on the project early on and cautious investment in trials and prototyping, this hideous project failure might have been avoided.

NOTES

1. Shih, W., Kaufman, S., and Spinola, D., *Netflix*, Harvard Business School, Cambridge, MA, 2007.
2. Christensen, C., *The Innovator's Dilemma*, Collins, New York, 2007, pp. 20, 23, 35.
3. Numerous sources; see for example John Pearson's Buckets Blog (http://urgentink.typepad.com), or Patnaik, D., *Wired to Care: How Companies Prosper When They Create Widespread Empathy* (FT Press, Upper Saddle River, NJ, 2009), or Schell, J., *The Art of Game Design: A Book of Lenses* (Morgan Kaufmann, Burlington, MA, 2008).
4. From http://www.biography.com. See also Dyer, J., Gregersen, H., and Christensen, C., *The Innovator's DNA*, Harvard Business Press, Cambridge, MA, 2011, p. 144.
5. Carroll, P.B., and Mui, C., *Billion Dollar Lessons: What You Can Learn From the Most Inexcusable Business Failures of the Last 25 Years*, Portfolio, London, 2008, p. 166.
6. Paraphrased from Capodagli, W., and Jackson, L., *The Disney Way*, McGraw-Hill, New York, 2007, p. 173.
7. See Butter, A., and Pogue, D., *Piloting Palm: The Inside Story of Palm, Handspring, and the Billion-Dollar Handheld Industry*, Wiley, New York, 2002, p. 76. Turns out the industry was far bigger than a billion dollars.
8. Corporate Design Foundation, Beyond techno gadget, http://www.cdf.org/issue_journal/beyond_techno_gadget.html, Sept. 30, 2010.

9. Berkun, S., *The Myths of Innovation*, O'Reilly Press, Sebastopol, CA, 2007, p. 73.
10. See Pachal, P., "Apple loses iPhone 5 prototype. Yes, in a bar," August 31, 2011, http://www.pcmag.com/article2/0,2817,2392244,00.asp, and Potter, N., "Apple iPhone 5 prototype lost in SF bar?" August 31, 2011, http://www.abcnews.com.
11. http://www.brainyquote.com; see also Carroll and Mui, *Billion Dollar Lessons*, p. 231.
12. http://www.merriam-webster.com.
13. Carroll and Mui, *Billion Dollar Lessons*, p. 232.
14. Catmull, E., "How Pixar fosters creativity," *Harvard Business Review*, September 2008, p. 4.
15. Mangelsdorf, M.E., "Good days for disruptors, an interview with Clayton Christensen," *Sloan Management Review*, Spring 2009, p. 67.
16. Lafley, A.G., and Charan, R., *The Game-Changer. How You Can Drive Revenue and Profit Growth with Innovation.* Crown Publishing Group, New York, 2008, p. 142.
17. Bloch, N., Gruver, K., and Cooper, D., "Slimming innovation pipelines to fatten their returns," *Harvard Management Update*, p. 4, 2007.
18. Mellow, C., "The rise and fall and rise of Iridium", *Air and Space Magazine*, September 2004.
19. Motorola and the Iridium flop, http://www.inovationzen.com.
20. Carroll and Mui, *Billion Dollar Lessons*.

7

Spreading the Ideas for Adoption

Ideas are easy. It's the execution of ideas that really separates the sheep from the goats.

Sue Grafton, author

An idea can be as flawless as can be, but its execution will always be full of mistakes.

Brent Scowcroft, former U.S. national security advisor

In April 2011, Waterloo Ontario's Research in Motion (RIM) launched the long-awaited Blackberry Playbook, RIM's offering to the fast-growing tablet market. A year later, the Playbook made up less than 2% of the tablet market, far less than former co-chief executive officers (CEOs) Mike Lazaridis and Jim Balsillie had predicted in premarket hype.[1] What went wrong?

Essentially, everything did.

The Playbook was announced in September 2010; it created substantial interest among the tech and business community based on the features promised by RIM and those expected in a RIM product: high levels of security and push e-mail. The actual launch did not happen for eight more months while various bugs were sorted out. During that time, Apple launched the iPad 2 less than two weeks after its press release in March 2011, and Samsung announced the summer launch of its Android-powered Galaxy Tab 10.1. So, while the

Playbook team fussed around with its launch, competitor products were arriving. Many potential Playbook customers got impatient and crossed the street.

Looking at the design of the Playbook, it would appear that RIM also had difficulty identifying the target market. Who is the customer, and what does the customer want? The concept of a tablet computer has been around for a number of years, but until recently the available technology meant nothing but clunky products with limited applications were available. In the last several years, internal circuitry shrunk, bringing out netbook computers and their short reign, but touch screens and LED (light-emitting diode) displays really facilitated the tablet. Apple's first iPad launched in 2010, and the market was immediately infatuated. Tablets from Apple (the market leader), Samsung, HP, and others are now prevalent, while the netbook market, the initial device filling the void between smart phones and laptop computers, has dried up.

First-to-market companies have the luxury of developing and launching a product or service that defines the market rather than asking customers what they want. Apple obviously did this with the iPod, convincing us quickly we needed a device that would hold 1,000 songs. RIM did it themselves with mobile e-mail on the first Blackberry back in the 1990s. I remember being initially skeptical about the need for picking up my e-mail when I was away from the office, but it quickly became invaluable. In this case, the iPad defined the tablet market. It was both a consumer and a business device, managing e-mail (including viewing attachments), calendars, and contact lists with visibility far greater than any smart phone. While the keyboard is not full size, it is more functional than using your thumbs on a Blackberry or iPhone. Add a Bluetooth keyboard, and you approach laptop functionality. Where it really defines itself is with videos, games, and the social or consumer side of its operating capabilities. Facebook, YouTube, and Internet functionality are quick and convenient, to the point that many users now rely on their home computer far less often, gravitating to the nearby tablet.*

---

* For more on this trend, see Appendix 1.

Android and Windows devices launched quickly, replicating the basic functionality of iPad. The devices all did some things a little better or a little worse than their competitors, each with advantages, but all very good.

Then, along came Playbook. Dubbed as a "professional-grade" tablet by RIM executives, from its late launch in 2011, it was clear that it underdelivered on basic functionality compared to what the market expected. Yes, it had video and games and browsed the Internet nicely, but where was the e-mail function? Playbook was launched with no resident e-mail capability, something basically invented by RIM, necessitating the chunky use of Blackberry Bridge on a nearby Blackberry smart phone to access your e-mail, calendar, and contacts. As a result of being late to market with their device, a market that had been defined by earlier products, Playbook failed to meet the needs of consumers and business users alike in a quickly changing environment.

Finally, RIM failed to appreciate the impact of developing and launching a completely new product line inside an existing organization. Tablets are different from phones and deserve distinct resources unencumbered by issues with existing products or services offered by the organization; they require separate development teams, dedicated project management, and unique marketing resources. As the cadence of multiple launches all came together through 2010 and 2011, however, resources were shared across platforms, teams struggled to hit dates, and deadlines were missed. There were 2,000 employees laid off in the summer of 2011, including enterprise marketing people responsible for getting the Playbook message out to corporate clients. A lack of accountability reigned among project teams, knowing they would not hit project deadlines but knowing some other group would perform *worse* and take the pressure off them.[2]

In the pre-Christmas sales season of 2011, half a year after their launch, Playbooks were offered in numerous markets for $199, less than half the cost of a similar Android, Windows, or Apple device. Competitors smiled as RIM sought to get more devices to the market in front of the release of operating system upgrades that would get them close to competing products. Finally, on January 23, 2011,

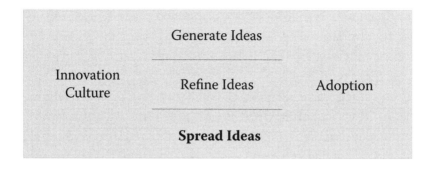

Figure 7.1 The innovation framework: spreading ideas for adoption.

co-CEOs Lazaridis and Balsillie resigned, replaced by Thorsten Heins, a RIM executive since 2007.

The Blackberry Playbook case highlights the three areas of focus we have when driving the development and *spread* of our ideas in the market (Figure 7.1):

1. Launch well
2. Know the customer
3. Commit the right organizational unit to the idea

You will recall our model from Chapter 5 (Figure 7.2 here) for reviewing ideas generated for the firm, now overlaid with the elements of the innovation framework. We obviously do not have the resources to utilize or implement all ideas before the company, and all ideas are not worthy of the time and investment necessary to launch them.

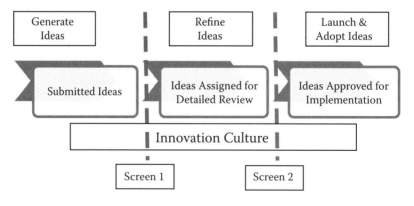

Figure 7.2 Idea development, review, and implementation in the innovation framework.

Those that meet organizational criteria, however, become projects. We are saying that the ideas that emerge from this framework deserve to be developed—they are part of the future of the company.

LAUNCH WELL

Projects are a number of things to the company, but they are primarily the embodiment of strategy. Projects bring strategy and vision to life for a company. They are the physical manifestation of managing change—heavy words for what started out as a simple idea.

My colleague, Dr. Kathryn Brohman, an associate professor at Queen's School of Business, and I have worked with several dozen different organizations over the last five years in the area of project leadership and execution.* Many firms still put the onus of project success on the shoulders of the project team. We have found that firms that struggle with managing projects and executing the launch of an idea run into issues in one of two areas: They fail to prioritize a project appropriately and commit the right resources or fail to allow for the uncertainty of the project in their planning. I elaborate both deficiencies further.

We ask several questions of leadership that help us determine the maturity level of their project organization: Can you identify the key point of contact on any company project? Can the project manager identify the executive sponsor of the project? Does the project manager and his or her team have a clear understanding of organizational strategy and, more important, the role their project plays in the strategy of the organization? How is that appreciation of corporate strategy reaffirmed on an ongoing basis?

Mature project organizations, companies that habitually launch well, recognize that project failure more often than not falls on the shoulders of leadership, not the project team. The answers to the questions just given should tell us that leadership has a continuing involvement in projects or even beyond involvement to the point of

---

* Kathryn and I are attacking the innovation challenge from both ends of the stick; while I am focusing on the innovation and creativity perspective, her research is leading to a book of her own on execution, due out in 2013.

commitment. (Sometimes, a leader will ask what the difference is. I remind him or her of the breakfast metaphor involving bacon and eggs: In that breakfast combination, the chicken is involved, but the pig is committed.) Someone at the upper management level of the organization owns that project. As the sponsor, he or she reaffirms the project's connection to the vision of the company on a continual basis. This person deflects other demands on the project team and knocks down the bureaucratic and organizational barriers that bog down a deliverable. The sponsor not only holds the team accountable but also ensures that the firm supports the project team. The sponsor fills a key role in the execution of any idea in the firm's innovation pipeline.

For this relationship between sponsor and project team to be effective, however, the organization needs to have a keen sense of a project's priority in the overall scheme of things. Innovative companies have a number of projects, often dozens or hundreds, on the go at any one time. Even with an ideal cadence between projects where resources are not being pulled in different directions by several project teams, competition exists for talent, funding, space, facilities, and time (even with the support of Lean). A key element of success, then, is to rank the projects in order of priority to the company. Put simply, which projects are more important to the company than others? Without that sense of priority, the battle for resources becomes political, with the result often being that one sponsor or one project gets the access wanted based on who or what they are rather than the nature of the project. Organizational competition is very real. Priority is put on the wrong project, or worse, there is no prioritization of projects.

Ranking projects can be an emotional and arbitrary exercise without some sort of framework. For most of us, something simple is enough to put structure around the project portfolio; we do not need to rank 15 projects first through fifteenth. Try this: Imagine a bucket of money that represents the overall project budget over the next 12 months (if your firm is involved in shorter-duration or longer-duration projects, adjust the horizon accordingly, but one fiscal year is a good place to start). We divide that bucket into three sections with horizontal lines as we see in Figure 7.3. The projects

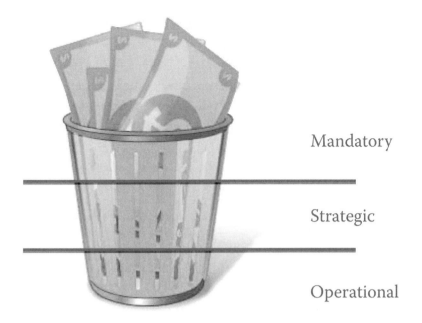

Figure 7.3 Project prioritization.

in the portfolio are then dropped into one of three categories: man-datory, strategic, and operational. Mandatory projects, as you have figured out, are compulsory and must launch in the time horizon pro-vided. They may have a regulatory component, like a Sarbanes–Oxley implementation; have a health-and-safety aspect, such as a new air purification system in a hospital; or be a customer-funded project with a fixed launch date. Mandatory projects by definition get the highest priority in the company.

Strategic projects (also referred to as high value/high impact in some companies) are viewed as key to the vision of the organization. Often, they have a customer or market focus but are always linked to managing core change in the company. These are the exciting proj-ects, project teams and people want to be part of them, and really they are where most innovations in the project pipeline would be categorized: They define careers and set the table for *Next*, often in both the company and the industry.

"Operational" projects are also important, or they would not get access to the resources necessary to develop and launch them. In this model, however, they are the lowest-priority projects. We may not have the resources necessary to launch all the operational projects in this period, resulting in some projects being deferred. Further, and more important for those projects in development, if we need to reallocate or move resources to a mandatory or strategic project that is in a pinch, we would pull those resources from an operational project.

We needed to resurface an aging parking lot at one facility in the late 1990s as it was filled with ruts and holes as a result of years of transport truck traffic. But, customers did not see that area of the plant, and funds were needed elsewhere, so that project got bumped several years in a row.

The mechanics of this do not need to be complicated; as an idea emerges from the pipeline and becomes a project in the organization's portfolio, it gets ranked as mandatory, strategic, or other. The right ranking for a project builds urgency within the organization around the idea, not only at the project team level, but throughout the company. As Scott Berkun said in his book, *Making Things Happen,*[3] execution depends on having a clear sense of what is most important. Picture a hand reaching into our bucket; as projects are funded, the hand has to reach lower into the bucket and eventually hits bottom, where there is not funding for any more work. Some projects get passed over this year.

The other advantage of this process relates to resource development. A firm can use operational projects to train project teams, moving team members to higher-priority projects as they develop.

The other cause of project failure we consider is that of underappreciated project uncertainty. If projects could be defined well at the outset—that is, we could accurately forecast time, cost, resources, outcomes, and test results—any project team worth its salt should be able to manage and launch most projects they come up against. There is the rub: We cannot accurately predict all the scenarios involved in the evolution of most strategic projects. These projects embody some of our best ideas, our organization at its most creative. Therefore, the project is "new." It is different from the stuff done before and involves uncertainty that can throw many of the project's elements to the wind. If we are realistic as an organization about the project we are planning

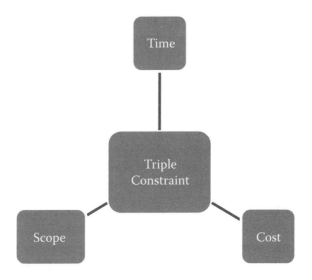

Figure 7.4 Triple constraint.

right now, how can we reasonably expect to pin a date and budget on this thing and launch it on a Tuesday, 18 months from now?

We cannot. And, this is where Kathryn Brohman and I work with a bit of a different definition of failure in our project environments. One of the fundamental tenants of project management is the triple constraint, or iron triangle, the relationship between a project's time, cost, and scope parameters (Figure 7.4). Many of you have seen this and understand the implied trade-offs—you cannot speed up a project without increasing cost or reducing scope. You cannot add content to a project without increasing time or cost. There are exceptions to the rule, but that is the basis of the triple constraint.

The problem is, this simple pyramid has been accepted as having too much weight in the definition of a project's failure. Research groups and organizations who study projects apply a "project success" grade on a project only if it hits all of the projected cost, time, and scope criteria. If the project is over time, over budget, or misses the scope, it is deemed a failure. In some studies, two-thirds or more of our projects are considered failures.[4] If there were indeed that level of project failure in industry today, we would still be driving horses and buggies and reading by oil lamp in the evening. We completely agree that the majority of firms struggle (in many cases mightily) with launching projects, but we generally get through it. Many of these cases are what we call a failure in the project management system of the company, not a failed project. Most of us agree that we could launch better, but we get there in the end. If it sounds like I am splitting hairs, here are two examples I use when speaking on the subject.

The Sydney Opera House was completed in 1973 at a cost of just over $100 million (Australian dollars), roughly 15 times its original budget and years late. By the traditional metrics, we would consider this project a massive failure. Consider what the Opera House means to the city of Sydney and in fact to the country of Australia, however, and we get a different picture—it is part of the image of the country and one of the top tourist attractions in the city. Flash back to the 2000 Olympics and how the image of the Opera House appeared several times in every broadcast. Postcards, travel magazines, and Web sites of the area all center on the Opera House. It hosts 1,500 performances per year, which are attended by over 1 million people, and in some media surveys has been called one of the seven wonders of the New World.[5] The stated goals of the project at its inception were to create a theatrical venue for large performances and an architectural concept making it one of the great buildings in the world. Against those goals, and the global recognition and appreciation of the structure, most of us would consider this a successful project.

As we dig into it, we find that the project changed drastically from what was conceived and planned initially by the city of Sydney. A design contest (won by Danish architect Jorn Utzon) weeded through 200 concepts submitted from around the world. Construction started in 1959, but translating the spirit of Utzon's design concept into reality proved complicated and time consuming, so progress was slow. Government changes, public criticism of cost overruns, and other issues led to Utzon resigning midproject, creating further challenges for the project.[6] Through stubbornness or foresight, however, the structure opened to much fanfare on October 20, 1973, at a ceremony presided over by Queen Elizabeth II, and many of the project issues faded from memory.

Compare this to another challenging project, the British Columbia Fast Ferry Project.* Commissioned by the B.C. government with the intent of stimulating new shipbuilding work for local shipyards; reducing congestion around the ferry terminals in Vancouver, Victoria, and Nanaimo; and reducing the travel time between Vancouver Island and the mainland, three catamaran-style ferries were built between 1995 and 2000.† When the three ships were completed, they came in at over double the original project estimate of $210 million and were three years late. The excess cost and timing, however, were the least of the project's worries.

Despite input (and, in fact, warnings) from experienced fast ferry shipbuilders and experts from other parts of the world, the consortia associated with this project underengineered the propulsion systems for the ferries, resulting in higher fuel costs and engines being strained when the ships ran at speed between ports. Airflow around the decks of the ferries was unreasonably warm, keeping people and their pets inside during transit, which was disappointing with such beautiful coastal scenery. Loading of heavy trucks onto the ferries was slow as the trucks' collective weight had to be balanced on the catamaran hulls. Perhaps worst of all, when the ferries did hit their designed cruising speed of 35+ knots, the ships created a wake that was large enough to damage wharves and coastal property.[7] Picture your dog barking at the ferry, only to see poor Duke (my mental image is a yappy little Chihuahua) washed out to sea by the boat's wake. The resulting outcry only exacerbated the disappointment in the overall fast ferry program.

In the end, the fast ferry program was cancelled, and the boats were auctioned off to the Washington Marine Group for $19 million (for all three ships, versus a cost of over $400 million) and have since been sold to the United Arab Emirates.[8]

It is quite obvious that this project was a complete failure and fittingly resulted in the provincial government being voted out in

---

* Fast ferries typically travel at speeds between 25 and 50 mph, versus 20 mph or less for traditional ferries. According to http://www.wiseship.biz/ferryspeeds.html, there are over 1,200 fast ferries currently operating around the world.
† Colleagues at an organization I spent some time with quoted windows and doors on this project.

the next election. The project was over time by three years and over budget by $250 million. It failed to achieve its stated objectives and was never able to achieve market success. As the case was debunked, it became apparent that failures abounded through the development of the project from concept to a ship in the water. Expert input from fast ferry shipyards in other countries was offered but ignored, denying the project the advantage of a sounding board and the ability to refine the design concepts based on solid experience. No prototype was built, which perhaps was not practical, and no existing fast ferry vessel was leased and trialed in British Columbia coastal waters, eliminating any low-cost experimentation. Think of what would have been learned by just renting a similar ship for six months. Perhaps it was naiveté, but more likely hubris or overconfidence, and the political rush to get the project launched before the next election, but it ultimately becomes what I refer to in leadership discussions as a hideous project failure.

Our projects have due dates, budgets, and content criteria, but they also have markets. The triple constraint in Figure 7.4 is really intended to outline the trade-offs between those three criteria: time, cost, and scope (or project content). That is, changing one or more of the elements impacts the other elements. The triple constraint should never be the sole judge of a project's success or failure without considering the impact of the project on the market place. Ultimately, do our customers want the new product or service created by this project? Project planning needs to be fluid enough to meet changing circumstances associated with its uncertainty.

More important than our appreciation of what project failure means is what we do about it. How do we manage the uncertainty and prevent a project from going south on us? As you can imagine, we are not talking about the roles or responsibilities of the project team here. This is not about the work breakdown structures or the Gantt charts or other mainstream project management tools. We are looking at the leadership of the organization, and when it gets down to it, most real project failures result from a breakdown in the project systems at the leadership level. When we look beyond Gantt charts, budgets, and other tools employed by project teams everywhere, where does leadership come in? What tools does leadership employ to facilitate an environment where projects succeed?

The leadership tactics we have found most successful here are as follows:

- **Gate reviews and other project visibility systems.** For example, in a gate review, cross-functional leadership groups meet with the project teams at key points in the project. The project team updates leadership on the status of the project, spending time on any developing issues or risks and its plans to deal with those issues. At the end of the presentation, leadership decides the fate of the project: The project proceeds according to plan through the "gate" to the next phase; it proceeds to the next phase with changes to the original plan; it holds at this gate until some issues are resolved; or the project is shut down as it is apparent the project will no longer deliver the value intended when it was initiated.*

- **Project sponsors and committed leadership support of a project.** Project sponsors are members of the leadership team and "own" projects. They eliminate barriers to the project's success and facilitate the project's development through its life.

- **Risk management systems**, where risks and barriers to a project's development are identified at the onset of the project, and mitigation tactics are deployed to eliminate or reduce the risk's impact on the project. For example, see the failure mode and effects analysis (FMEA) process in Chapter 6.

- **Actively communicating how a project supports the vision and strategy of the organization.** This is part of selling the project to the organization, connecting people's work to the goals of the firm, and an ongoing responsibility of leadership.

If this sounds like a lot of work, it certainly is, at all levels of the organization. It takes time and money for the organization to launch well on a regular basis. We are holding everyone accountable for the

---

* There is an appropriate piece of wisdom from the Dakota aboriginal people. The Dakotas used to say, "If you are riding a dead horse, get off."

success of this new initiative. At the end of the day, however, if we have deemed an idea important enough to launch and indicated that it is part of our strategy going forward, is it not worth our time as leadership? What could be a more important use of our time?

KNOW YOUR CUSTOMER

We have circled around the subject of knowing your customer in a number of ways throughout the book. While discussing Lean, we looked at the concept of value and understanding what our customers really want and need from our organization, with the goal of eliminating the complexity that bogs our processes down and keeps us from focusing on that value equation for the customer. In the *idea* process, we focus on the needs of the customer as we look for novel ways to deliver that value. We *refine* those ideas with models and mock-ups the customers can hold in their hands, see, and touch, enabling them to begin to place a value on the idea.

Our focus here is a bit different now that the idea is crystallized. At this point, knowing our customers means understanding how we will get the idea into their hands. What are their expectations for timing, packaging, and delivery? Most important, who *is* the customer? As we have discussed, one of the biggest reasons for an idea not being adopted in the market is the organization failing to identify the target customer. Identifying the customer is straightforward when the idea is incremental or a new generation of an old product. With platform or disruptive ideas* such as tablet computers, however, we are creating new markets with customers all their own.

If we go back to the smart phone market for a minute, we can consider how the customer groups were reasonably distinct until some time around 2010—there was the consumer category and the professional or business category. Each had needs that were common, such as calling, calendars, and address books, and each had unique requirements, such as e-mail for professional users and

---

* Platform and disruptive innovations are generally accepted as ideas that create new consumer space. As well, disruptive ideas change the way the existing space operates and attracts new customers.

photographs or MP3 music files for consumers. Blackberry owned the professional group, with its secure "push" e-mail, file compression for reduced bandwidth requirements, and security, while Apple, Motorola, and Nokia dominated the consumer markets with great styles and functionality.

Somewhere along the line, the distinction between user groups blurred and now is virtually gone. Business users are on Android and iPhone devices, and consumers have been using Blackberries for some time. New Blackberry designs targeted consumers, with students and nonprofessionals carrying a Blackberry because the keyboard facilitated texting. Android and Apple kept focusing on the user, with enhanced browsing capability, great cameras, and video, to the point that professionals also wanted the phone bling—think of the business executive you know who used a Blackberry for work but had an iPhone for personal use. There were thousands of these people who carried two competing products. Lawyers and finance people kept the Blackberry for thumb typing long memos and briefs to clients but had 300 songs loaded on the iPhone for personal use; they finally started to realize, "This is stupid," and pushed back at work, demanding a choice. Why are we lugging two phones around, paying twice the carrier fees when one will do the job? Corporations everywhere are killing their Blackberry-only policy and adopting architecture to support Android and Apple devices.

Whose market is it, anyway? Time will tell, but the concept evolving in this discussion is that companies create markets and not the other way around.* There was no smart phone market before RIM created it. It started off with a focus on the business customer but has evolved to be all of us because of the effort by firms like Samsung and Apple. Now that the market is established, innovations inside the market are incremental—faster processors, higher-resolution cameras (eight megapixels now on my Galaxy, far better than the original digital camera with two megapixels my wife and I bought

---

* Perhaps this contradicts market-driven economic theory. The discussion may feel chicken-and-egg like, but the logical sense of it to me is that the company creates a service, and the market adopts it or not. Need may have been there but was not manifested until supply was created.

10 years ago), high-definition (HD) video, impact-resistant designs, and of course, access to growing app markets. Within this market-place, we are competing for scarce customers because that market already exists and has been defined. Companies will grow as more people get smart phones, and companies will disappear as they realize their ability to attract customers versus the competition is limited. Within a couple of years, two or three companies will own most of the market as it exists and compete on diminishing profit per device sold—until the next product creates a new market, again.

So, how did RIM identify its target customer when it created the smart phone market 15 years ago? Another way to ask the question would be, who needs access to e-mail everywhere, all the time, but just does not know it yet? For RIM, co-CEO Jim Balsillie worked tirelessly to meet with bankers, lawyers, and executives every-where to get devices in their hands and help them understand the value of being connected. He was part evangelist and part techni-cian, working with the users to see how they interacted with the early Blackberry, taking those observations back to partner Mike Lazaridis to refine their concept to appeal to a wider audiences. These customers were busy, engaged, and connected—Balsillie had to do the work to get the product in front of them, but they drove the next phase of adoption for RIM. Colleagues, fellow commuters on the train, and travelers in airports would see the device in action and think, "That is something I have got to have!" Knowing their target customer allowed RIM to leverage them; indeed, that category of customer has been the most loyal to Blackberry over the years, even under some of the current pressure.

You may remember first-generation Blackberries were just slightly larger than a credit card, with a small keyboard and a screen that let you see two or three lines at a time. An improved version followed shortly, enhancing both of those features based on user input and observations. What you may have forgotten is that the first several versions of Blackberry did not have an integrated cell phone; they were an e-mail-only device. RIM did not target cell phone users as their customer market; it went after people it thought would want to be connected via e-mail and created what became the smart phone market as devices and features became integrated.

Here, customers are part of both our refining and launching process, as we hone in on who the market really is for the innovation. Picture something as simple as pizza. What does the customer really want in a pizza? For many of my university students, it is about cost and access: Where can I get a reasonably priced pizza at 3 o'clock in the morning while I finish this term paper or walk home from the pub? The pizza company that locates near a campus, keeps costs low, and delivers 24/7 will do very well with that crowd.

Some customers are less sensitive about cost but want that pizza to be hot and fresh. Being close by, then, can be cost prohibitive in a larger market where we need numerous stores to manage the population. What if we broke the paradigm and developed a mobile kitchen? Rather than investing in a number of storefronts, let us buy a half-dozen vans, equipped with smaller coolers, counters, and a propane-gas-fired oven. Calls from customers come in to our 800 number or Web site and are routed to the van closest to that location. We prepare and bake the pizza on the way to the customer's address and pull the pizza out of the oven as we pull into the customer's driveway. What could be hotter and fresher than that? The vans restock at a home base a couple times per night, but that location does not have to be prime retail space, just central and efficient.

Another category of customer wants a custom experience with the pizza. The challenge here is that the current model only lists ingredients as words or sometimes pictures on a menu. Incorporating an idea from another restaurant business, what if we let customers select their crust, toppings, sauce, and cheese from containers of ingredients they can see and almost touch, as the fast-food company Subway does it? Build the pizza and then grab a table and a beverage and your pizza will be along in 10 minutes. Maybe we install a couple of big-screen TVs to entertain the customers while they wait.

When we start to think about the customers—who they are and what they want—it becomes much easier to satisfy their needs. In the examples, I think we could charge a little more at the same time. Everyone wins (and I am getting hungry thinking about it).

COMMIT THE RIGHT ORGANIZATION

We have all had the experience of being pulled in several different directions at the same time. That is part of life. It happens; we deal with it and move on. Within the early life of an innovation, however, it can kill an idea. Former chief technology officer at Cisco Judy Estrin speaks regularly on innovation and authored a book *Closing the Innovation Gap* in 2008. In Estrin's garden analogy,[9] ideas in their early stages need to be nurtured and developed and given the opportunity to grow in the organization. At the same time, the garden does not have the space for all of our new ideas; some need to be pruned.

If we think back to the idea pipeline in Figure 5.3, we recognize that not all ideas are developed in our company. Logically, they cannot. We do not have the resources to launch everything, even in a Lean world where we have freed up people, time, and funds to focus on what is most important. There are too many ideas, and if we are honest about it, not all of the ideas are good ones. Said another way, some ideas win, and some lose. If our idea won, someone else's lost. We have to appreciate that in most of our firms, there will be people who push back against ideas and initiatives we have in development. Whether they were part of the idea that lost or have other issues, we know there will be people who are not supportive of the direction this idea takes the firm.

My colleagues Dr. Peter Richardson and Dr. Elspeth Murray call this the 20-70-10 rule, where 20% of the team will be enthusiastic and supportive of the new idea or direction, 70% will sit on the fence, and 10% will actively push back and resist change. In their book, *Organizational Change in 100 Days: A Fast Forward Guide,*[10] Murray and Richardson suggested three tactics to deal with the apparent division in ranks inside our firm. The first 20% are easy; they are already engaged and on board. We need to involve them in the plan and utilize them. Doing so will help convert some of the fence sitters in the 70%. Sometimes, the people in the 70% and 10% categories just need to be heard. Here, we need to tell the story of the innovation, talk about why it fits and connects to the vision, and then open the floor. Let them ask questions; there are probably some very good concerns that could help us refine and launch the concept better than if we had not heard them out. In most cases, the 70% will move in the right direction.

The 10% who resist the change can be a significant challenge, but we have to deal with them. Talk to them, let them vent, ask questions, but do it in smaller groups—do not give them the floor in town hall-style meetings. Get specific: What is it about our plan that does not work for you? In some cases, acknowledging their issues will help convert the 10%, but in some other cases you have to move on. Dealing with them may mean moving them to a less-critical part of the operation or, as a friend used to say, give them the chance to find gainful employment somewhere else. Regardless, we cannot let that group detract from something we see as a core part of our future success as an organization.

One of the challenges faced by RIM with the Blackberry Playbook was resource allocation. Resources from different projects and departments were pulled to the Playbook launch, involving people who had nothing to do with Playbook or had numerous other responsibilities, and Playbook was just one of them. As a historically innovative company, RIM has a number of significant projects on the go at any one time. In the last two years, that has included the Playbook tablet; new versions of Blackberry Curve, Bold, and other smart phones; and a significant new operating system, Blackberry OSX. Project and engineering resources in a company like this are generally partitioned, in this case into smart phones, tablets, enterprise systems, and software (and smaller, more focused teams within those categories). We talked about prioritization being critical to the success of a launch for a company—identifying a project as core and critical and then staffing and supporting that project to fruition. So, what happens when we say smart phone X is a priority, but we keep asking for resources from that team to support the tablet project? Smart phone X is no longer as important as the tablet. Therefore, work, effort, and morale slips; the project is delayed, and the quality of the product and launch will be reduced. RIM saw this in spades through the launch of Playbook, where engineers were given multiple, conflicting assignments. Sales and marketing teams were instructed to push Playbook in their discussions with enterprise customers, therefore neglecting smart phones, RIM's bread and butter.

We prevent this situation by creating a dedicated team for the new product or service. Applying Lean principles from Chapter 2, we free up the personnel and resources we need for the new group, and that project is their home (in this way, Lean enables innovation *and* execution). They own and are accountable now for that project. Sometimes, we locate that team in a different facility, give them a different reporting structure, and let them grow and evolve as the new business needs and not subject to the existing paradigms within the larger business.

The key factor here is the recognition that the new, disruptive idea will be a challenge in some ways for customers to identify and adopt, but it will also be a strain on the existing organization to support. By setting up a distinct operation to develop and launch the idea, we avoid the distractions and resistance in the existing company. I was part of over 30 product and service launches while working in industry, and the most challenging by far were those that seemed outside our traditional comfort zone.

There are benefits outside our current operations to this process as well. New firms do not have to play by old rules. This thought usually applies to a new competitor in an existing business, but we can think the same way when we move into adjacent markets with a new idea. Not only are we developing a new product or service, but also we can experiment with new organizational processes or structures at the same time, something more agile, or perhaps more customer centric, ideas that can be spun off and applied back to the parent company.

The key here, obviously, is to size the organization to the size of the market and let it grow as we identify more customers. We also need to acknowledge that we may not yet have the innovation in its best form for growth. Getting the idea "right" at this stage is actually not as important as giving ourselves the ability to react quickly to feedback from the early adopters of our idea—think Microsoft and its model of launching software and then coming out with a patch or revision a couple months later when glitches were identified by the user community.

Ultimately, launching the idea well drives adoption, and adoption is where the value of the idea is realized. Some ideas can be sold or licensed, or perhaps tabled for another time, but until we get the ideas in the hands of our customers, the idea is just that. Identifying the right customer group and launching well allows us to create a market, which is something innovative firms do: They create markets and industries.

EFFECTIVE LAUNCH: CROCS

When we look at the most significant innovations of the last decade, the ubiquitous Croc shoe has to be in the top 10, at least as far as its impact on its market, ranking up there with iPods, social networking, and Under Armour athletic wear. Revenues for the Croc firm were just over $1 million in 2003, the first year for the company, but rose phenomenally to $355 million in 2006. Very quickly, Crocs became the shoe that you saw everywhere.[*] Many people owned several pairs of the indestructible, funky clogs. That kind of growth out of nowhere deserves some attention in any discussion concerning innovation.

But, the innovation is not really what you think it is. Sure, the shoe had a unique design, resisted odor, and did not slip on wet surfaces. It was very comfortable for people standing for long periods or slip-on convenient when you were heading out to the grill to flip your steaks. Yes, the Croslite™ resin was core to the product, and the shoe design and colors attracted attention everywhere, but the real innovation that launched Crocs was in their supply chain, and like many of our other Lean Innovations, it was borrowed from other industries.

Crocs was founded by three friends, Scott Seamans, George Boedecker, and Lyndon Hanson, who resold the Canadian-made shoes from a warehouse to sailing aficionados. The three partners quickly realized the enterprise was going to be big and recruited college friend Ron Snyder to run the organization for them. Snyder, formerly of contract electronics manufacturer Flextronics, convinced

---

[*] There are few style points on which I will take a stand, but I will say that I have never owned a minivan, had a mullet haircut, or owned a pair of Crocs.

the trio that Crocs needed to own the material and technology associated with the shoes and get big very quickly.

In the broader apparel market, including shoes, order cycles tend to be very long. Orders for the fall line were placed in late winter or early spring, and spring collections were ordered in the fall. Shoes and clothing were produced in bulk, sometimes six months before they made it to market. As a result, forecasters for apparel retailers had to be very good at predicting what styles, colors, and materials were going to appeal to the market six months later. Think of the risks here, assuming we have products consumers are looking for—if we underestimate the market, our goods are sold out early in the season, and consumers clamor for more. We can order more from suppliers, but it will take three to six months to replenish our inventory. Retailers are upset because their customers want something they cannot supply; consumers give up and move on to the next available option. If we overestimate the requirement and market demand does not materialize, we are forced to take advantage of that retail innovation, the outlet mall, and dispose of our excess inventory at a fraction of our cost. That is the traditional supply chain model in the apparel industry, and most companies work with it. Companies like Zara and, as we will see, Crocs, which get innovative with that supply chain model, tend to do very well.

Snyder realized that the unique styling of the shoe was going to be subject to the laws of the trend, and that Crocs had to take advantage of market appeal and demand while it held. To really take advantage of customer enthusiasm, Crocs had to continue to get shoes in the hands of retailers as quickly as possible when demand was witnessed. So, Crocs went about reinventing the shoe supply chain in the manner of contract manufacturing, as in Flextronics, where Snyder and his handpicked executive team previously worked. Snyder and his team said that if consumers and retailers wanted more Crocs in that season, they would get the shoes into their hands (and on their feet!).

Crocs bought the formula and production assets from the Canadian firm making the original Crocs and then proceeded to get that raw material produced in several locations in the United States and Europe. From there, it was compounded in Italy and sent to manufacturing locations that eventually included Canada, China, Europe, and South America. In many cases, Crocs was buying capacity from the supplier, not shoes, enabling them to flex the production requirements based on what the retailers' inventories and customer demand looked like. When retailers were running low on the women's pink size 7 Cayman model, they were able to call Crocs, and the mold for the size 7 Caymans went in the press. Inventories were replenished within days and weeks, rather than months.[11]

The ultimate benefit to the market, and therefore Crocs, in this case was the availability of the shoe to whoever wanted it. Prices stayed strong, demand was fulfilled, so volumes soared. In the traditional order cycle, retailers would have had to wait until the next season for order replenishment, and the opportunity and possibly market access may have been lost. Consumer tastes are fickle, and something else may have been the next big thing months later. As well, the shoes are pretty simple products, and as we have seen in the last several years, subject to the clone market of knockoff manufacturers. Snyder's strategy of ramping up production capability quickly and buying capacity from a number of in-house and third-party suppliers enabled the company to launch well and get the product in the hands of all interested customers extremely quickly.

Where Crocs struggled over the subsequent period was in having no follow-up act after its penetration into the shoe market.[12] The problem, if it was a problem, was that the shoes last too long. The resin resists odor, the shoes are durable, and really, how many pairs of Crocs do you need? After satisfying that initial run up in demand, the market was looking for something else from Crocs, but the idea tap had run dry. Unless the business strategy is to get in and get out quickly (not unheard of), organizational prosperity depends on continuous innovation, which we focus on in Chapter 8.

NOTES

1. Castaldo, J., "Who the hell is responsible for this anyway?" *Canadian Business*, February 20, 2012, pp. 46–52.
2. Ibid.

3. See Berkun, S., *Making Things Happen: Mastering Project Management*, O'Reilly, Sebastopol, CA, 2008. This is a well-written book offering lots of suggestions not only for the project management team but also leadership in the organization.

4. See Standish Group's *Chaos Report*, published every few years. Also see interpretations of these reports in places like *CIO* magazine, http://www.cio.com: Levinson, M., "Recession causes rising IT project failure rates," June 18, 2009, http://www.cio.com/article/495306/Recession_Causes_Rising_IT_Project_Failure_Rates_.

5. See, for example, Whitelocks, S., "The all new 7 wonders of the world," May 31, 2007, http://www.telegraph.co.uk/news/uknews/1553152/The-all-new-seven-wonders-of-the-world.html. It appears that there is no governing body for the seven wonders of the world, resulting in several categories, such as the seven wonders of the modern world, seven wonders of the architectural world.

6. Bourne, L., "Avoiding the successful failure?" PMI Global Congress, Asia-Pacific, Hong Kong, January 29–31, 2007.

7. "B.C. to auction off fast ferries," *Canadian Press*, January 9, 2003, http://www.ctv.ca/ctvnews/Canada/20030109/bc_fast_ferries/030109.html.

8. "B.C. fast ferries' voyage to oblivion lead to Middle East," *Vancouver Sun*, July 30, 2009.

9. Estrin, J., *Closing the Innovation Gap: Reigniting the Spark of Creativity in a Global Economy*, McGraw-Hill, New York, 2008.

10. Murray, E., and Richardson, P., *Organizational Change in 100 Days: A Fast Forward Guide*, Oxford University Press, New York, 2003.

11. Mui, Y.Q., "Crocs Shoe Company stumbles during recession," *Washington Post*, July 16, 2009.

12. Caldwell, R., "The downside of overnight success," *Canadian Business*, November 9, 2009, p. 99.

Embedding Innovation for Long-Term Growth

8

Back to Culture

The greatest real thrill that life offers is to create, to construct, to develop something useful. Too often we fail to recognize and pay tribute to the creative spirit. It is that spirit that creates our jobs.

Alfred P. Sloan, former chairman of General Motors

What was the best thing before sliced bread?

Author's quotation

Do you remember your first digital camera? Ours was a Canon Digital Elph, with a 2.0-megapixel processor in it. It was small and heavy and the screen on the back was about an inch across, barely able to display pictures we had taken with the camera in a visible size. When you turned the digital image into an actual printed picture through the local photo depot, you could not print it larger than a 4 × 6 inch image, or it was grainy and of very poor quality. Vibration (slight shaking of the camera when you took a picture) was an issue but was not evident until you developed your pictures. We loaded many of the images on our computers and e-mailed some of them, but bandwidth and Internet speeds were still young, so that was also a cumbersome process. Such was the nature of preliminary digital photography.

Consider its evolution. Even photography enthusiasts and professionals have been using digital now for years. Film and film cameras are virtually unavailable in all but specialty stores. Cameras now included in our phones, computers, and tablets are superior to anything on the market 10 years ago and are capable of taking stills and video and of easily editing them in seconds.

Given that Kodak was one of the founders of digital camera technology in the early 1970s, we would expect it to be a major player in this market. Sadly, the company filed for Chapter 11 protection from creditors in January 2012, and one of the iconic brands of the last 100 years teeters on the edge of vanishing.[1] How does that happen? How does a company that develops *Next* in its industry fail to adopt it and direct the course of the firm and that of its competitors?

In hindsight, it is easy to question the leadership of the organization, who failed to seize the opportunity, failed to see the proverbial writing (or in this case, photos) on the wall, and failed to adapt. We often look at disruptive innovations like this and say that leadership was too focused on existing markets, that current success and a focus on today's customers kept them from seeing the prospect on the horizon. In Kodak's case, however, it was already threatened as Fuji had begun making significant inroads in its paper and film business, a market Kodak had long owned. There should have been more urgency around the conference room table in Kodak's leadership meetings. Perhaps hubris, perhaps inertia, but without being a fly on the wall in their executive chambers over the last 40 years, it is difficult to decipher. What is clear, however, is that a culture for innovation in Kodak was virtually nonexistent.[2]

In the interest of clarity, we need to revisit a previous discussion for a moment. In my mind, and many others on the subject, there is a big difference between innovation and research. Kodak spent millions on what they called research and development (R&D), although it really was not R&D. It did the research, but how many of those concepts developed in R&D were brought to market? In fact, a significant part of Kodak's strategy as it struggles to reinvent its business in the Chapter 11 proceedings is to raise funds through the sale of thousands of patents. There are so many things wrong with this picture that it is tough deciding where to begin. That it had the ideas but did not pursue them is unfathomable, especially considering the pressure it was under in the market. That it believes

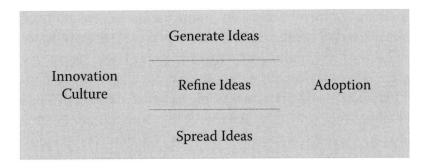

Figure 8.1 The innovation framework.

a competitor may be interested in buying Kodak's patents is very curious, as those competitors likely have their own technology and are less interested in propping up a failing Kodak regardless.

In my model (Figure 8.1), innovation includes the implementation of an idea, its commercialization if you will. R&D by itself generates the new knowledge, but that knowledge has little or no value until we bring it to market through spread and adoption. Innovation creates that value for the firm. Kodak, in telling its scientists and engineers to keep digital technology on the shelf, was stifling innovation.

At the time of its inception in the 1970s, the market was obviously not ready for digital picture technology. Personal computers were still a dream, and there was no simple way to share or even store images. Film technology and imaging were far superior, digital was nowhere close to being a threat, and while we are at it, Kodak was making a lot of money from film.

Since we know how the story turned out, what would it have taken at Kodak not only to lead the charge as digital emerged over the next 20 years but also perhaps accelerate it? Where in the firm do we look for that inspiration? The solution begins when we circle back to our culture, but not to our culture alone, as there are other factors as well. Think back to our opening vignette in Chapter 1 involving the oil markets, OPEC (Organization of Petroleum Exporting Countries), and the lack of any substantial initiative toward seeking alternative fuels. The culture of the organization (or society) at the time was such that there was no significant drive toward seeking *Next* in fuels and energy.

Within Kodak, there also was no culture for innovation, no curiosity or drive to see what the company was truly capable of delivering.

Perhaps a more appropriate term of reference is fear: There was no fear at Kodak that something would come along and actually shake the foundation of its business.* How sad that the game-changing technology was within its four walls the whole time. For me, a leadership perspective has a healthy dose of paranoia present in any long-term planning process. Remember the three characteristics of capable leadership? We recognize opportunities, we avoid catastrophes, and we break paradigms. Avoiding catastrophe goes far beyond just risk management; it also encompasses a realization that there is something out there that will trip me up. I am not paranoid; someone really is out to get me (and my market share). Once we realize that, the fear itself can be inspiring and help drive the culture of the company toward innovation.

Let us change industries (slightly) and look at the movie and DVD rental business for a moment. We spent some time previously on Netflix and how Reed Hastings and company refined their initial DVD-by-mail concept into a workable model and a multibillion-dollar business over a 10-year period. The growth in that market came at the expense primarily of companies like Blockbuster, which hung on to its investment in retail locations, limited inventories, late fees, and part-time sales help. When DVD-by-mail rental appeared on the market, Blockbuster executives were quite public in their position that the new business model would not appeal to consumers, and they would stick with their existing strategy. Why wouldn't they? Blockbuster was very profitable at the time, growing its customer base and opening new stores all over North America as more people invested in quality home entertainment systems and DVDs became broadly available.

Therein again is the challenge with disruptive innovations: The incumbent firm more often than not is unprepared to deal with the appearance of a new model, fails to adapt, and begins saddling up the horses for its ride off into the sunset. These firms may possess some

---

* My friend Steve Mercer refers to this as king-of-the-hill complex.

culture for innovation, but it is typically incremental at best: in this case, new store layouts and décor, multiday and weekly rentals, video games, and member loyalty programs. Look at us go now.

A firm with a genuine culture of innovation goes far beyond that; it looks at the horizon for opportunities and threats. It rewards creativity and embraces challenges. It takes the approach that if something is going to threaten our business, it may as well be us that initiates and controls the innovation. Such was the approach by Netflix when video-on-demand (VOD) emerged around 2005. The firm had already Leaned out the previous model of video rental with its Internet-based DVD business. With VOD, however, Netflix recognized that the technology had the potential to replace its business model that relied on hard media with DVDs. What were its options? The DVD-by-mail business was still growing; we could say that it was still in the early majority stage (Figure 8.2). Netflix could continue to grow for several years, remaining profitable for the foreseeable future. Hastings himself had built and sold a company prior to Netflix; perhaps now was the time to sell the business and move on to the next big thing. Or, it could take the position that if someone is going to develop and commercialize the next innovation in home entertainment, it was going to be Netflix, and in a classic case of trial and error, that is what it did.

Initially launched to customers with Xbox and other gaming consoles, Netflix launched limited VOD availability in 2008. Supporting

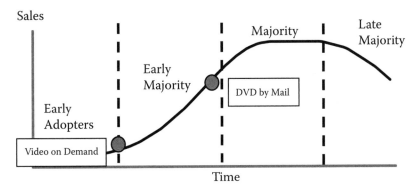

Figure 8.2 The Netflix service life cycle.

technology was still developing, but feedback from early adopters helped it fine-tune the process while it negotiated access to certain movies and television series. Releases were never current, as the studios protected their theater business by delaying digital releases and remained concerned over piracy and payment for anything digital. Netflix encountered its share of turbulence along the way, most significantly with the failure of its Quikster initiative in 2011; high pricing for VOD alienated many of the customers Netflix had worked so hard to develop over the years.[3] Evolution in the VOD market is happening very quickly, with the networks themselves developing strategies and Apple's iTunes always on the threat board. How it shakes out over the next five years is the territory of guesswork, but I would not bet against Netflix in some form or other; the young firm embodies the spirit of an innovation culture, willing to cannibalize its own revenues in the pursuit of *Next* in its industry. In effect, it was creating a new service life cycle while its current model was still growing (Figure 8.2). How many of us as leaders would have the courage to do something similar?

Apple has demonstrated its willingness to cannibalize an existing business unit over the years: iPhones include music and many other capabilities of iPods; as sales of iPhones increase, they will have an impact on the sale of iPods. iPad tablets are doing the same thing to MacBook computer sales. This is the evolution of innovation in a firm with a strong creative culture.

Saying is one thing, but doing is something altogether more difficult. As we look back over the last 100 years, only a handful of companies have truly reinvented themselves. IBM no longer makes computers; 3M is a long way from its Minnesota Mining and Manufacturing days; Johnson & Johnson and GE have evolved. Are there many others? How does your firm compare?

Business failure is not likely in the strategic plan for most firms, agencies, and organizations. Highlighting failed organizations such as Kodak or Blockbuster as an example of a firm's destiny is not my intent. Rather, those are examples of leadership teams that failed to recognize the opportunities in front of them and were consequently unable to adapt as the market changed. Think of firms like this as occupying one end of a bell curve, with companies like Apple on the other end. Most of us are going to be in the middle somewhere, living in what I call the salad bar. Think about it; few of us get excited about eating a salad. Picture a friend who says, sitting down in the restaurant, "I'm going to have a great big salad!" This is not likely. We eat salad because it is nourishing, and it reduces the guilt of eating what we really want, a nice steak, a small rack of ribs, or even the vegetarian fajitas.

As an organization, we cannot aspire to be salad. It does not really matter what you do to the salad; it is still an appetizer, roughage, or an add-on, occupying the lower-cost portion of most menus. Innovating on the salad bar is incremental at best; let us add walnuts, cranberries, (shudder) gorgonzola or blue cheese, or perhaps a side of grilled chicken. Incremental improvement is fine for existing operations and business units in the company, but it rarely excites existing customers or attracts new ones. We need something new. Fusion cuisine, for example, or farm-to-table dining; restaurants can be and are innovative. Customers will pay for the next big thing.

With disruptive innovations, you do not need to be the first mover, but you do have to move. Had Kodak or Blockbuster reacted, it would still be in both games. These companies did not possess an innovation culture. Let us talk about what an innovation culture looks like for the rest of us.

Innovative organizations embody most, if not all, of the following characteristics, all of which are simple; these companies:

- Think about tomorrow's customer, even while they serve and focus on today's, recognizing that their business will look very different in 5 or 10 years.
- Constantly review their product or service life cycle(s).
- Challenge current assumptions in their business.
- Are risk takers, yet are smart about it. They seek to navigate the minefield, not avoid it altogether. Some ideas will fail, but they do not allow themselves to be paralyzed by fear.
- Collect and review ideas from numerous sources.
- Consider *Next* in the goals and vision of the organization.

- Have leadership that recognizes that *different* is okay. They recruit for fresh perspectives and new approaches. They create environments where people can think and behave differently (like an *i-space*).
- Look outside their industry for inspiration, building elements from diverse organizations into something that changes the game in their business.
- Are agile and lean, unencumbered by more than a minimum amount of complexity and process. Leadership, employees, and customers alike all understand the business goals, direction, products, and services.

The idea of recombining existing elements within our stable does not always resonate with leadership in many organizations or even occur to management. CBS, for example, was not only a broadcaster but owned the world's largest record store. It seems natural that it would launch a music video channel when that wave arrived in the early 1980s, but CBS missed out to MTV.

Gillette had all the pieces for a battery-powered toothbrush in Duracell batteries, Oral B toothbrushes, and Braun electronics but was beat to the market by products from Arm & Hammer and Philips.[4]

Research in Motion was the innovation and technology darling in portable communications for a decade but drifted in recent years as it struggled with product complexity and failed in several launches.

It is a pretty small circle of companies that embody the culture of innovation we have discussed here. The obvious question, then, is how do you make your company more innovative? How do you drive a culture of innovation in a firm that has existed in your current model for a long time? This gets back to leadership (again). Your culture comes from leadership; your behavior, beliefs, attitudes, and styles within the company. You influence and embed culture with how you reward and compensate people. What is the discussion like around the water cooler or in the lunchroom? What is your meeting culture like? Are the management meetings in the same place at the same time? Do you and your colleagues all sit in the same chairs every week? Is the agenda always the same, starting, say, with the financials? "Johnson, let's go through the numbers." Sound familiar? Is the *work* of the business getting in the way of people innovating?

Driving *Next* in our business takes a focus on a framework like I have described in this book, and I start that framework with culture. For me, it has always been the most important part of managing change in a business, so we start and end the book with a focus on culture. And, we change culture by starting with a change in our behavior as leadership. I am not talking about a drift from our core values or the vision of our business; I am advocating a new approach to how we walk and talk around the firm, that is, our day-to-day behavior. Have some fun with this.

BC'S INNOVATION CALISTHENICS

1. Shake up your routine.
2. Take a new route home.
3. Turn off your e-mail.

My innovation calisthenics are expanded in the following pages.

Shake Up Your Routine

Think about that management meeting we just discussed. Maybe yours is at 10 a.m. on Friday every week. Agenda, chairs, location—all are the same. A few people get there early, most are on time, but there are always a couple of stragglers who roll in and mumble a quick apology before sitting down and dealing with an e-mail on their smart phones. Some people look at this and say this meeting culture is a fact of life; everyone is busy, we are cramming 20 pounds of potatoes into a 10-pound bag. The meeting is important, but we have a lot of stuff going on, so we multitask. As a result, that meeting has limited value. You get people's attention for only a portion of the meeting; people are anxious to move on to the next thing or deal with a different problem. In fact, people are so familiar with the meeting that they know when they have to pay attention and when they can tune out. This is sad, but true for many of our meetings that have been on the calendar for an extended period of time.

To deal with this phenomenon, the simplest thing to do is to change the meeting: move the location, use a different time slot, and especially, shake up the agenda. As I write this, an early spring has hit Ontario, and everyone is itching to get outside. Let us hold the meeting outside at the picnic tables this week. This is not a perfect meeting environment, but the fresh air will be good for us. Moving the time slot is a challenge the first time, as everyone has other meetings that can conflict with this one. Give people a couple weeks' notice, especially if you are changing the day of the week along with the time. When you walk into the meeting, sit in someone else's chair.* Watch his or her reaction on entering, reading a Blackberry, and then looking up at you with a stunned expression while he or she figures out what to do. This is small stuff, but we need to get people out of their comfort zones sometimes, and this is an easy start.

A friend who is the chief administrative officer for a municipality distributes agendas prior to meetings and suggests attendance is not required if you cannot add value to the meeting. If that sounds too good to be true, the "stick" is that repetitive absence could indicate that you are not really needed in the organization. Show up ready to add value.

With the agenda, why not start off with some customer matters first rather than the finances? Invite someone from customer service or a supplier to give a 10-minute update on what is going on in his or her world. People like me do short (and long) speaking engagements with company leadership teams all the time to kick off or wrap up their annual meetings with a new theme.

From our launch and execution discussion in Chapter 7, you can wrap a management session around a project gate review and let the project team get some face time with senior leadership. Not only is it beneficial for them, but also it keeps you current on where a project stands.

The key with this exercise is perspective and awareness. Messing with people's schedules, environments, and silly things like where

---

* Another link to farming? In olden days when dairy cattle were returning from the pasture before milking, they would be guided back to the barn in a very systematic fashion. Daisy will always be in the stall to the left of Alice, and Betty was to the right of Annabelle. If they were not in the right place, there was chaos.

they sit wakes them and us up. The veil of efficiency that we have been operating under lifts and allows us to see more of what is going on around us. We also can take this beyond the meeting schedule.

Look at the office layout and how your teams are arranged. If people have been in functional areas for as long as you can remember, try a pilot where a group of people are arranged according to the product or service they provide or the customer they support. The best case is often where you can arrange a cross-functional group of people in one area and build off their differing perspectives. Look at some fresh paint on the walls or different flooring. When it feels different, people will act differently.

Get a coffee with someone in the office you do not get a chance to talk to that often; see what that person's interests are outside work. Make a habit of connecting with someone different every day.

There is a story from General Motors (GM) in the early 1990s that is a great example of this tactic.* GM was driving a significant cost push with its suppliers and put a man named Jose Ignacio Lopez de Arriortua in charge of the initiative. To fill in the scenario a bit, GM had been under incredible pressure for a number of years. The recession of the 1980s had a long-term impact on its sales and profitability. Combined with intense pressure from the Japanese and German car companies and renewed efforts from Chrysler and Ford, GM was struggling. In 1991, it lost $4.5 billion. To turn this around would take a new way of life as the old ways obviously were not working. Even GM's attempt at Lean with programs like Targets for Excellence were not enough.

Enter Lopez and what he called his purchasing "warriors."[5] To turn GM's financial situation around would take, among other tactics, major savings with its supply base. Picture the following scene: Lopez was in an amphitheater with hundreds of GM purchasing staff. The charismatic Lopez stepped on the stage and talked about the pressures on the company. He was honest, discussing the billions of dollars GM had lost over several years and how his "brother,"

---

* My apologies to those of you who were automotive suppliers during that period. My intent was not to make the nightmares return.

chairman Jack Smith, had charged the purchasing team with fixing the problem. Then, he looked down at the contract in his hand, a multimillion-dollar agreement with one of their suppliers, and said that while GM was struggling and living on bread and water, suppliers were getting rich, and he ripped the contract in half. "We are at war!" he yelled. Again and again, he mobilized his purchasing team, one group at a time, bringing them together for a series of tactical and motivational meetings before releasing his warriors on the supply community. He ripped up contracts, literally. He forbade his warriors from eating junk food, saying only a diet of fruit and rice was appropriate for those in battle. He told everyone to take off his or her wristwatch and put it on the other hand. He wanted people to realize that they had to behave differently if they were to succeed in their mission to "save" GM. Wearing their watches on the other hand would remind people several times a day that this time it was different.

As the situation evolved, this was not a good time to be a supplier. Some stopped doing business with GM, but most stayed, or tried to, making less money. The "Lopez era" became personal for many companies; some sued GM for breach of contract. Lopez himself led many plant tours at suppliers, "helping" them find ways to reduce costs and in turn pass those savings back to GM. Contracts were reopened after a supplier had done the design and engineering work on a project, and multiple suppliers were invited to bid on that project. All new contracts were awarded in an auction-style bidding process by which any supplier in the world could tender a project—GM's version of eBay.

Some say that Lopez started a chain of events by which suppliers would reluctantly do business with GM, but they saved their best technology for companies like Toyota or BMW. While his initiatives saved over $3 billion for GM between 1992 and 1993, it is fair to say they had a much broader impact on the industry. Ultimately, this culture shift and the practices implemented by Lopez did not save GM, just postponed the inevitable, with the company declaring Chapter 11 in 2009.

Such change is possible in any business, but it starts by changing the way we work. The true measure of a culture is how it endures over time; in this case, many of those same purchasing tactics and the culture between GM and its suppliers exist 20 years after the departure of Lopez. The upside, perhaps, was a forced focus on Lean for many North American suppliers that had little reason in the past to apply those tools. GM, Ford, and Chrysler all applied their own version of cost pressures through the 1990s that necessitated all suppliers to optimize their operations.

Changing our routines is the first step. We see things we have not seen or noticed previously. We pause, reflect, and start to smell the opportunities. We are aware again.

Take a New Route Home

Admit it! You like to take the same route to and from work every day. You have optimized it over the years, and your car can almost drive itself. You know that if you time the traffic lights perfectly, and everyone is moving well, you can get home in 37 minutes. On those days, you pull into your driveway, put the car in park, hit the remote to close the garage door, and then think, "How the heck did I get here?" You have been on autopilot the whole way home, and you have not had a single new thought the entire time.

This is also me. Whether I am heading over to the university or just going to the rink for hockey, I get into a pattern, which can mean I miss a turn to another destination if my mind settles into the university or rink route mode. The challenge we face here is one of efficiency: Efficiency is fine for when we need to be efficient, but it comes at the expense of creativity. Connecting to our discussion in Chapters 2 and 3, we all have the ability to be creative, but we do not spend enough time being creative. It really is the balancing act depicted in Figure 8.3.

The objective of this part of the calisthenics is to see things that we are not normally seeing. It connects and supports the first of the calisthenics in that it is one of the routines we are breaking up, but it is more about exposing ourselves to other sights, inputs, and ideas. Our awareness is up, and now we capitalize on it by putting ourselves in unfamiliar environments. The drive home is just one of those environments, where you will see people, signs, buildings, and activity that just makes you think. Some of that exposure will lead to an idea or concept that you had not thought about previously.

Figure 8.3 Efficiency versus creativity.

Look also at what you read. Most of us subscribe to a couple of magazines and read a newspaper during the week. As a new reader, it takes us a couple of issues to get familiar with the layout and where to find what we are seeking. Once you have settled in, you look forward to that quiet time when you can read it. After a while, however, maybe a period of months or even years, the magazine becomes repetitive and familiar. That was a situation I ran into with an excellent Canadian financial publication. It has great columns on investing, personal finances, real estate, right down to renovations on your home or the best credit card for your circumstances. The problem was that after a few years, all the articles started sounding the same: this year's top mutual funds, their "couch potato" investment strategy (which is a winner), top cities to live in, and so on. All were good, but I had seen them. The subscription had a three-year useful life for me, but I just renewed for three years beyond that before I shut it down, and the last dozen issues were just skimmed.

It is the same with a newspaper or whatever else you regularly receive. Most editors look to shake up the delivery and content as best they can, but that can only be incremental innovation, nothing really "new." To really get a fresh perspective, we need to read something new—a different newspaper (although its political theme will be different from what you are used to), a different magazine, a different news program or Web site on your tablet. These will all expose you to new perspectives and ideas. Even if you do not agree with all of them, those perspectives make you think.

Back at work, most of our organizations have subscriptions to industry periodicals; for a car parts manufacturer, that could be *Automotive News*; an accounting company will have finance or related journals; a consultancy may bring in *Harvard Business Review* or a link to *Ivey Business Journal*'s online edition. All are good, but also very traditional—we are still living in the salad bar, while the articles themselves call for a spicy pasta dish.

What if you bought a couple of unrelated subscriptions for the lunchroom: *Golf Digest* or *Home and Garden* magazine? These would be interesting and welcomed by employees, cheap at less than $50 per year, and encourage people to troll for new ideas and perspectives, especially the idea of understanding what our customers want or what their interests are.

Turn Off Your E-mail

Turning off your e-mail is a strange one for many people I speak with and probably the area of greatest resistance. At the same time, it has some of the greatest opportunity for change within today's companies. Go back 15 years, before Blackberries, and think about how you occupied your day. You had meetings, activities, phone calls, and travel. You were busy, but you got it all done. When you went home at the end of the day, you were generally done, other than perhaps a call or report to deal with after dinner.

Today, we are never unplugged. The upside (and the value proposition of a Blackberry or iPhone) is that when we need to have access to information, an e-mail, or an issue, it can be accessed, 24/7. Sitting in the airport is now productive time whether you use your Galaxy phone or the airport's free Wi-Fi with your laptop. How quickly the culture of dealing with e-mail "now" has permeated our society and blurred the work/leisure balance. On vacations, at social outings, even sitting in a movie or the theater, you see (or worse, hear*) people dealing with a call or e-mail—look how productive we are now!

---

* There are few things more intrusive than hearing one side of a cell phone conversation in a public place.

The problem is that e-mail makes you stupid, and the nice folks at King's College in London University have the data to prove it.[6]

In a study in which participants were given a series of tasks to do while managing their e-mail on a nearby computer, King's College measured the participants' productivity and performance on those tasks. When an e-mail came in to the computer, the participant had to drop the task, respond to the e-mail, and return to the task. You can appreciate what happened; it takes time for us to ramp up to our previous level of performance on a task when we are interrupted. In the case of the experiment, we are looking at 10 to 15 minutes to ramp up to full capability again, which King's College was able to equate to a drop in IQ of 10 points—10 points! Some of us cannot afford that kind of hit to our intelligence, but we are doing it to ourselves on an ongoing basis, every day. As an addendum to the experiment, the controllers measured the impact of smoking marijuana on intelligence and saw a drop of only four points (clearly, research funding in the United Kingdom is different from what we can get away with in Canada). So, e-mail makes you stupid, more stupid, in fact, than smoking pot.

What do we do about it? I can hear some people heartily suggesting we ditch the e-mail and give everyone marijuana; think how satisfied and creative your employees will be! Make smoke, not spam! Good luck with that.

The real opportunity is some discipline. What I am advocating, and a number of companies are now doing, is to manage expectations around e-mail. This is dead simple and something you would hope your people are doing already, but few of them are. Start by advising people that they are no longer expected to respond to e-mail between the hours of 1 and 3 p.m. on Wednesday afternoons or some other relatively innocent time in your calendar. Put the Blackberries on "silent" and leave them on the desk. Do not schedule meetings during that period if you can avoid it. Give people those two hours to be completely productive. At first, it will be an adjustment (one executive said his office looked like a group of addicts in withdrawal; another said he kept getting calls from outsiders: "Did you get my e-mail?"), but after a few weeks, people settle in and appreciate the time to get things done or focus on something new. At that point, you can add Mondays and Fridays, then afternoons between 1 and 3 p.m. all week. Afternoons have quickly become an "e-mail-free zone," and people get back to managing their e-mail instead of letting it manage them. They check in at planned parts of the day, perhaps right before lunch and before they head home for the day. They are productive and empowered, more in control of their time and schedules. More work gets done, and people have time to focus on other things.

What if something urgent comes up? Well, they can call you or (gasp!) come and see you. When I talk about this concept with a group of managers, I hear about people working in these companies that e-mail back and forth with coworkers in the next cubicle or office rather than standing up and talking to them, or people's frustration with the overuse of "reply all." E-mail is a good medium for information, agendas, or updates, but it is a lousy way to communicate. Let us build some controls and expectations around it again and use it for what it is. Stop letting it manage us, reduce our productivity, or interrupt more important activities in which we are engaged.

This is another perspective on Lean: What is the most important thing for me to be focusing on right now? Maybe it is a meeting, a class (ask me how I feel about undergrad students on Facebook in a lecture), or a dinner with friends. Whatever it is, it certainly is not my e-mail. The link back to innovation on this is the massive culture shift we get out of freeing up people's time and focus. When they need to execute, they are more engaged and capable; it gets done faster and in most cases far more effectively. Performance goes up. When execution is dealt with, people have more time for the other side of the fulcrum—innovation. Remember from Chapter 2, a significant obstacle to people's ability to innovate is the perception of a lack of resources: people, funds, space, and ... time. Free up the time, and they can get there.

Performance should also go up as the increased face time results in stronger relationships and fewer misunderstandings as a result of an e-mail gaffe. How many of us would like to retract an e-mail we should not have sent?

Culture shifts are difficult—indeed, they are tantamount to turning the direction of an ocean liner—but they can and do happen all the time. Think about something as simple as a sneeze, a reflex really, that takes place in fractions of a second. Until about 10 years ago, we would sneeze into our hand or a handkerchief or tissue if one were available. The health profession advised that this was not sanitary, and with fears of colds, flu, SARS (severe acute respiratory syndrome), and other infections, people began sneezing into their arms. It took some practice, but people were able to adjust a reflexive habit they had built over a period of decades. Try sneezing into your hand next time you feel the urge building; it is tough.

Look at how we have all adopted e-mail, smart phone technology, and especially social media like Facebook or LinkedIn. Talking on our smart phones has also changed; in many states and provinces, it is now illegal to talk on a cell phone while operating a vehicle without a Bluetooth device.* That behavioral shift will happen within a year or two across North America.

In its purest form, shifting the culture of an organization is about managing change. Without a culture for innovation within our firm, we have no hope of a sustainable focus on innovation and therefore no real chance of thrilling current and future customers with what's *Next* in our business. The next question in our culture shift is, who leads it?

The obvious answer is our leadership team. As I have said, we get the behavior, values, and focus we demonstrate every day with *our* behavior. For this to really resonate and embed itself in our organizational culture, however, it needs to become objective, measurable, and visible to our employees, customers, and other stakeholders.

How do we demonstrate that commitment? The first step is to identify the innovation champion within the organization. Who is

---

* Progressive provinces like Alberta, Canada, have built this into a "distracted driving" law, which includes reading, shaving, doing makeup, or cutting your fingernails while driving. Sound bizarre? You have seen people doing things like this (and worse) while driving. Legislation is even being considered that would make it illegal to walk and text or talk, it is hoped to prevent people from walking out in traffic while thumbing a message. Natural selection anyone?

the person in our leadership ranks who "owns" or should own innovation? There needs to be a central, empowered focus on innovation that we can identify. In some cases, the choice for an innovation champion is obvious, but if not, I list several characteristics that can help the process:

- Innovation champions are senior, respected members of the team.
- They have the character, confidence, style, authority, and drive to initiate change and fresh approaches and sponsor new ideas.
- They realize there is no "box"; they think differently, which we see in some of the off-the-wall comments or ideas they present in discussions.

Back at Autosystems, that champion was my friend Jason Bonin, who certainly had no place for boxes and restrictions. I recall one conversation during which the leadership team was considering how to reduce the particulate contamination in the coating operations of our production facilities. We were already operating at a Class 100 clean room level* but wanted to be better. The question was, How do we get better than that? "Well, you're looking at membrane technology," was Jason's response. Most of us were stunned, and then we laughed. Of course, none of us had heard of membrane technology. A company needs that type of inspiration.

Whatever title we use for the innovation champion (chief innovation officer, vice president of development and innovation, or something less formal), his or her role in supporting and driving innovation in the firm is clear and broadly understood throughout the company.

Our commitment is also demonstrated in how we support the learning and development of innovation capability through the organization. We cannot just state we need to be more innovative without helping the team get there. It is hoped you have seen throughout

---

* Class 100 clean room levels permit no more than 100 particles greater than 0.5 micron per cubic foot of air. Ambient air has something like 1.3 million such particles per cubic foot. (Source: http://www.coastwidelabs.com.)

the book and in the businesses where you have worked some of the roadblocks or obstacles to innovation and creativity, so what will you do about this? As the innovation champion, would you sponsor innovation training for key people in the organization and, best case, help them get to the level where they could train others across the firm? Would you insist on employees having broad access to the tools of innovation, regardless of their position? Could you formalize your commitment to innovation with a planned series of innovation events throughout the next quarter or year?

Some firms that contact me about innovation training never get beyond the point of looking at their calendars. We look at dates sometimes six or seven months out, and they cannot find one or two days when they can get people together or, worse, get senior leadership to commit to the dates. Sure, they are busy, but with their actions they are saying that innovation is really not the priority they think it is. Free up the time and make it happen!

What we start to see with this culture shift is more of our "organizational time" being spent on the creative side of the scale shown previously. Execution and efficiency are what today's customers are buying, certainly, but we need to spend time on tomorrow's customers as well. Maybe we are never in perfect balance here, but our creative side is starting to permeate the culture and environment of the company. You will know you are on the right track when you hear people in meetings discussing some new idea or concept, and instead of saying "that won't work here," the question is, "How would we get that to work here?"

Part of our organizational commitment to innovation is demonstrated in how we measure it. A lot of firms look at their patents applied for per year or approved per year. That is good if you are a science or technology firm, recognizing the patents alone are not innovation until they are implemented somewhere. Look at the new business units or revenue streams that are created every year and how many we are shutting down. What changes have we made to head count and resources associated with new products or services? When firms like 3M commit to a percentage of revenues coming from businesses developed in the last five years, factors associated with that commitment show up on their version of a balanced scorecard: How are we really doing with this?

We have discussed the *capability* for innovation and the *culture* that drives it. There is one final component that embeds the creative side into the fabric of our organization, and that is a *catalyst* (it even starts with a *C*, so perhaps we call this the three *C*s of innovation). We need some event or situation that kicks it into gear, triggering our activity toward innovation, and that catalyst can be internal or external.

If this is a new initiative and part of the new strategic plan for the organization, we need an initiation for the organization worthy of its importance. If we have acknowledged that we cannot stay the same and survive,* show people that. Use a town-hall-style meeting to talk about the pressures on the business, why we need to change, and what we are going to do about it. Talk about the training, the idea programs, or the projects we are launching. Connect the event to the core visions and strategy of the organization and then talk to people about their role in *Next*. Make the event feel different, perhaps in the venue or in how the message is delivered or who delivers it. Most important, follow up after the event with actions related to the message—an innovation jam or online idea forum. Acknowledge and celebrate some of the first successes the firm has achieved to continue the momentum.

Externally, the catalyst may be a threat from a competitor or some other change in market conditions. It could be related to the economy or society in a broader sense, demands from your customer, or even a policy change by a regulatory body. These inputs force us to think differently and, ultimately, to do something. Ignoring, say, the emergence of a new technology like Kodak did can literally kill the company.

Can you think of any evolving innovations or market factors that threaten or provide opportunity to your industry? Here is another way to look at it: If we ignore the opportunity, chances are it will become a threat.

It is fair to say that the culture of society as a whole is becoming more innovative than ever in history. New generations adapt to

---

* See Chapter 1.

change far quicker than the previous one. Contests are held and recognition is given to the most innovative companies. Google launched its Lunar X Prize in 2008, to be awarded to the first privately funded team to land a lunar rover* on the moon, have it travel 500 meters, and send back data (probably by Gmail). The prize is $20 million if the team can do it by the end of 2012, then drops to $15 million until the end of 2014, when the contest ends.[7] Netflix did it privately when Reed Hastings offered $1 million to whoever could improve their online movie recommendation algorithm. Sir Richard Branson did it in 2007 when he put up $25 million in the Virgin Earth Challenge to whoever can "demonstrate to the judges' satisfaction a commercially viable design which results in the net removal of anthropogenic, atmospheric greenhouse gases so as to contribute materially to the stability of the Earth's climate system."[8]

Fast Company magazine looks at the 100 most innovative companies; the Canadian Innovation Exchange (CIX) pronounces Canada's 20 most innovative companies annually. *Canadian Business* magazine and a panel of experts awards Canada's Most Innovative Executive as well. Many other journals and business magazines run similar evaluations, based on a set of measurable criteria, in some cases, the type of factors we may review on our internal innovation scorecard. Talking about our progress with innovation reaffirms the strategy, and the recognition for the firm in publications like this is extremely valuable when it comes to recruiting; people want to be around like-minded others. Tell the story and celebrate the victories.

So, here we are at the end. When I wrap up a program with a leadership team from a company, we have a discussion about what is next for the firm (lowercase "next" in this case). "Tell me one thing you will do differently upon returning to work tomorrow," and we go around the room. Some people have crystal clear ideas that they will do or try; others are still working with it, which is fine.

How about you? Some of you are innovators already and read voraciously on the subject looking for fresh perspectives. Others have taken the first steps and are moving their company strategy

---

* A sport utility vehicle (SUV) for the moon.

toward one committed to innovation. Now that you are at the end, or really, the beginning, what will you endeavor to do differently tomorrow? Here are a few suggestions:

On Monday, take a new route to or from work. Sit in a different chair in the management meeting. Ignore the Blackberry for a couple hours and tell your team members to do the same thing. Ask a customer what problem is keeping him or her awake at night and how you could help with it. Hire a farmer, a technologist, or a logistics expert—these people are all experts at figuring things out, solving problems, and thinking differently (if you have ever had to get a nonstandard package somewhere in eight hours, you know what I am talking about). Sign up for a course that has been in the back of your mind for too long now—put it in the front of your mind. Invite a speaker to your next executive retreat. Take a serious look at the complexity in your operations and eliminate some of it, one process or product at a time. Spend time with team members launching something important. Consider what your market will look like in 5 or 10 years and what role your company will play.

What will be the catalyst that drives the next innovation for you?

Recall our oil story from the beginning of Chapter 1. Oil prices were climbing. The chairman of OPEC was in the news talking about the fact that there was no market-based reason for the price of oil being where it was. Lots of committees and commissions were launched to investigate the situation and write a plan to do something about it.

In the end, little happened, and nothing really changed. Why is that? It really gets down to culture. In this case, the culture of the organization (our society at large) was not ready for the change. We have the capability to develop viable alternatives—no one doubts that. The catalyst in this case should have been the rising prices at the pumps. Perhaps prices did not go quite high enough to reach a tipping point and get our attention. But, we were missing that third leg on the stool: the culture to recognize that we need to do something about it. That solution, however, could be right around the corner; see the electric car vignette at the end of the chapter.

I am going to wrap up with an interesting quotation from a journal dating back a few years that may help put things in perspective. The scene illustrates a young Steve Jobs as the whiz kid founder and force behind the creation of Apple.

> But his vision of building a corporate counterculture in California's Silicon Valley ended in 1985 when Apple's management, responding to declining sales and poor morale, relieved him of his responsibilities. Like all personal computer manufacturers, Apple was hard pressed to fight IBM's dominance of the market.[9]

Oops. We know now that this story was not over. Things change, constantly. Both companies reinvented themselves; IBM sold its computer division in 2004 to China's Lenovo Group, and Apple went on to be arguably the dominant force in the personal computer industry. The executive teams that look for and lead that change with a clear view of what the customer wants will create new opportunities, markets, and industries. They will build a culture for innovation that embodies the way people in the firm think, talk, and act. They become the icons in their field.

If your organization ceased to exist tomorrow, would anyone notice?

As Aristotle said to me one time when we were talking: "Excellence is an act won by training and habit."[10] Without a constant drive for innovation in the very fabric and culture of a firm, the future is uncertain. If companies like Kodak can fail, other organizations such as Netflix, Research in Motion, and even Apple need a healthy dose of paranoia in their strategic planning. Do not wait to see what is *Next*; build it yourselves.

ELECTRIC CARS AND DISRUPTIVE INNOVATION

General Motors launched the first commercial electric car as the Saturn EV1 in 1997 after successfully demonstrating concept versions of the vehicle as early as 1991. The first generation of the vehicle sold just over 1,000 copies and was replaced with the second-generation EV2 for the 1999 model year. GM offered the vehicle only as a lease, which meant it maintained ownership of the car and could effectively take the expensive and high-tech vehicles back whenever it chose to do so. In 2002, it decided to do just that and recalled all of the outstanding leases, with GM CEO Rick Wagoner stating that it could not sell enough electric cars to make the program profitable. Naturally, the conspiracy theorists blame intense lobbying efforts by the oil companies for at least part of the responsibility in the EVs coming off the roads.

Electric cars have been around as long as those powered by combustion engines, with some scale models and early concepts being built in the early 1800s. The challenge with the vehicle has always been battery technology, which remains its Achilles' heel today. The size-to-performance relationship of the batteries has always been tilted toward heavy, bulky, and low range.

Hybrid vehicles, first introduced by Toyota with the Prius in 1997, overcome charging and range issues by complimenting the electric motor with a small gas engine. The onboard computer decides when each system will ultimately run, but by design, the intent is the gas engine is "off" while the vehicle idles and cruises downhill. As the vehicle accelerates, the engine restarts and remains running at cruising speeds. As a result, the Prius actually gets better fuel economy in the city than it does on the highway (44 mpg versus 40).[11] When the brakes are applied to slow the vehicle, the electric motor acts as a generator (dynamic braking) to charge the batteries.

Research continues in pure electric vehicle technology, as well as other engine systems such as hydrogen fuel cells and vehicles powered by natural gas. Government and some manufacturer incentives are in place to drive the sales of such vehicles as the hybrids by Toyota, Lexus, Ford, and Hyundai and the primarily electric systems such as the Chevrolet Volt and Nissan Leaf and others like them. Styling has improved, and the vehicles are really quite nice to drive, being very quiet while running the batteries, and the electric motors provide significant "oomph" on larger versions. So, what will it take to get more of us buying these cars?

The current states of these technologies are really still what Christensen called disruptive, meaning there are challenges facing the new vehicles, and the existing industry standards still dominate.

Commonly cited issues with hybrids and electric vehicles include the following:

- Cost. The Nissan Leaf, for example, is more than double the price of its gas engine twin the Nissan Versa.[12] One would have to do a lot of driving to make the premium worthwhile, even for a "traditional" hybrid where the premium is $5,000 to $10,000.
- Charging stations at home are expensive, at $1,500 or more,[13] and are still very uncommon at highway rest stops or other locations away from home.
- The vehicles have limited range on a single charge, typically around 100 kilometers.

So, *Next* in this case is not quite there. Gasoline engine technology continues to improve, with average fuel economies increasing with each generation of vehicle. Other critics have pointed out that vehicles relying on electricity are still using "dirty" energy, often deriving their energy from coal-fired generating plants. My response to all that is, so what? This is still a very new focus for most companies, and development can take many directions. These innovations will be refined.

Gas engines are a mature technology, with improvements that are incremental. Car companies will keep working on this, and I applaud their progress, but transformational improvements will be rare. Electric and hybrid technology is still emerging, really at the early adopter stage in the product life cycle. Innovations and improvement made here in the next 20 years will be huge, and I would be willing to bet that many of those developments will not be made by incumbents in the industry (as I write this, GM is scaling back production of the Chevy Volt due to slower-than-anticipated sales[14]).*

When he gave up his controlling interests in Magna, founder and former chairman Frank Stronach insisted on keeping a minority (yet controlling) stake in Magna's E-Car Systems, the company's electric

---

* Having said that, I would not bet against Toyota. Could it be one of the companies that reinvents itself to support new technology and consumer tastes?

car development organization. E-Car has partnered with Ford and is really the muscle behind creating the Focus electric car. Stronach and his partner, Fred Gingl, have also teamed up to create electric boats and bikes, but most of his efforts remain true to his roots on the automotive side.

Other companies are also doing it now, and some very interesting models are available in the market. Have a look at Tesla Motors in California. Tesla offers a small line of luxury performance electric cars that start at around $50,000 (after the $7,500 federal tax credit) to north of $100,000. Is that $100,000 for an electric car? Yes. By the way, it has nappa leather interiors and 21-inch wheels and gets from 0 to 60 mph in 4.4 seconds.[15] Tesla claims its Model S with the 85-kWh motor will have a range of 300 miles when driven at 55 mph, and it will charge on a common 110-volt outlet in your garage. The batteries will recharge in about five hours to full capacity and gain about 60 miles of range for each hour of charging—very cool.

We have the capability to innovate and develop commercially viable electric and other alternative propulsion vehicles. The culture will evolve as more of them become available, but what is really missing here is a catalyst to drive that culture of adoption and efforts to innovate *faster*. What that catalyst will be—a government mandate, extreme oil prices, new battery technology—we do not know, but we need to get used to the idea. *Next* is coming.

NOTES

1. Smith, A., and Hibah, Y., "Kodak files for bankruptcy," January 19, 2012, http://www.cnnmoney.com/2012/01/19/news/companies/Kodak_ bankruptcy/index.htm.
2. Moore, T., "Embattled Kodak enters the electronic age," *Fortune*, 1983. Republished by *CNNMoney*, January 8, 2012.
3. "Netflix stock falls after subscriber losses, failed Quikster spinoff worries investors," *Washington Post*, October 25, 2011.
4. Kanter, R.M., "Innovation: the classic traps," *Harvard Business Review*, November 2006, p. 6.
5. See "Hardball is still GM's game" by J.B. Treece, Z. Schiller, and K. Kelly. *Business Week*, August 7, 1994, or *Newsweek*, "GM vs. VW" by Michael Hirsh, December 8, 1996. I was also fortunate enough to

be in the automotive parts business at the time of the events as they unfolded at GM and their supply community over that span of years. The stories we heard directly from GM purchasing people (while they renegotiated our contracts) were incredible.

6. See, for example, Wainwright, M., "Emails pose threat to IQ," *The Guardian*, April 22, 2005, and Orlowski, A., "Email destroys mind faster than marijuana—study," *The Register*, April 22, 2005.

7. Pawlowski, A., "Google launches new space race to the moon," June 20, 2008, http://www.cnn.com.

8. Virgin Earth Challenge, http://www.virgin.com.

9. Doyle, K. and Johnston, A., *The 1980s: Maclean's Chronicles the Decade*, Key Porter Books, Toronto, 1989.

10. http://www.brainyquote.com.

11. http://www.fueleconomy.gov. A U.S. Department of Energy Web site.

12. McClearn, M., "Frank Stronach's electric Kool-aid," *Canadian Business*, January 23, 2012.

13. Ibid.

14. Higgins, T., "GM to scale back production of Volt," *Financial Post*, March 5, 2012.

15. Company Web site information, http://www.teslamotors.com.

Appendix 1: Fearless Predictions and Things to Create or Kill

I intended to have a bit of fun with this section. These are things I think about when I am driving down the highway between Quinte and Kingston or on the train to Toronto. There is no real place for this material in the body of the book, but they are ideas, issues, or problems I hope someone is tackling. If that is you, please give me a call. A few may sound like pet peeves; that is okay, as they represent a problem for at least one consumer out there—me.

In this section are my fearless predictions on changes to society or industry. I am in no way related to Nostradamus or the ancient Mayans. There is no Cross Calendar. I am speculating and could be completely wrong (but I do not think I am). Any correlation to actual events, names, or places is entirely coincidental.

If you have some ideas like this, let me know, and I will summarize them on my Web site (www.leaninnovation.ca).

HOME PHONES AND LAND LINES WILL DISAPPEAR BY 2020

Okay, you may have thought about this already. I picked the 2020 date because it has a nice symmetry to it. It will probably take longer than that for older generations to give up their phones. Most people on the planet have at least one cell phone now, so there is redundancy in the system already. There are other reasons to support the argument as well:

- Infrastructure investments and maintenance are far less expensive with cell towers than landlines.
- When you answer the phone at home, the call is never "for you," and you have to call someone else to the phone. That would not happen with your cell.
- There are fewer telemarketing calls on your cells (so far; please, please, please keep it that way).

Some issues and obstacles still exist for this to be a widespread phenomenon. Signal strength in the "boonies" needs major work (iridium anyone?). Costs need to come way down; in Canada, for example, cell phone bills are very unreasonable compared to other markets. And, we get back to the work-life balance discussion from earlier in the book.

THE NUMBER OF WRISTWATCH MANUFACTURERS WILL DROP BY 50%

From what I could glean from the Internet, there are something like 178 watch companies in the world right now. Some of these are part of larger parent organizations, so the actual number of watch entities is a bit smaller, but 178 is a pretty huge number. The problem? A good chunk of the younger generation tells time now with their phone. In fact, that phone is their timepiece, alarm clock, stopwatch, and obviously a lot more. Perhaps the number of clock manufacturers also decreases.

There are other contributing factors here as well. How many watches do you really need?* When you buy a quality timepiece, you

---

* My wife is rolling her eyes at that one. I kind of have a thing for watches (and sunglasses), so I probably own more than I really need.

like to wear it, so the others sit on your dresser. Watch technology and what it does for us really has not changed in the last couple of decades. Accuracy keeps going up, but how accurate does it really need to be? Citizen makes a great device that is powered by light—no changing batteries on the Eco-Drive. The Swiss have some great brands that have gone through a renaissance in the last 20 years. TAG Heuer, Rolex, and others are doing very well. But, with fewer people buying watches, and those watches lasting decades, sales will drop, and some of the fringe players in those 178 brands will have to disappear.

METER MAIDS/TRAFFIC TICKET POLICE/PARKING ATTENDANTS WILL NOT BE NECESSARY

I am not trying to eliminate jobs, but the lack of necessity for meter maids, traffic ticket police, and parking attendants involves some pretty simple technology. We are giving high-quality cameras away free in cell phones now, so why not mount them on the parking meters? When the time on the meter expires and an appropriate grace period has gone by (say 10 minutes), the camera snaps a picture of your license plate, and you get a ticket by e-mail. The same technology could work when entering a parking garage.

In Hong Kong and other areas, they use something called an Octopus card, which is really the first wave in the micropayment sector. Millions of people are using trains and transit in Hong Kong every day, and stopping in the queue to pay with money, credit or other forms of payment would be obstructive and time consuming. The Octopus card is preloaded with a fixed amount of money, so it behaves like cash, but you just flash it at the sensor on your way to your train without really slowing at all. In Canada, Tim Horton's is doing that now with its Tim Card, making it easier and faster to buy that donut. Most of our credit cards now have a "wave" feature: You just get the card close to a sensor, and it manages the transaction.

Something similar would work well in the parking systems of any city and could be more effective when snow- or dirt-covered license plates prevented a good picture. Flash your card to pay the meter or enter the underground lot. Attendants are not required, and the use of cash itself in society cannot be far behind.

DESKTOP COMPUTERS WILL DISAPPEAR BY 2017

I am giving this one five years and probably less in our homes. Laptop computers themselves will decrease in use as tablets become more effective; integration is already seamless with Bluetooth devices. At our house, we are on our iPad more often than the old desktop now. When we replace the central desktop later this year, it will be with a laptop connected virtually to our printers and the Internet through Wi-Fi. This is nothing new for most of you. The wireless setup is cleaner and allows people to browse or work anywhere in the house, including when they are watching TV or socializing.

Speaking of the TV, now you can get a "smart" television, and it will only get smarter. It will connect to your Wi-Fi, and you will be able to set it so that an icon will flash in the bottom corner when an e-mail or Facebook post comes in (resist the urge to do this; watch the game!). Your tablet or Bluetooth keyboard will allow you to use the TV as a computer from the couch. Think of what that means when you are connected with someone by video in stunning 3D high definition (HD).* Some service providers are already offering inter-active services by which incoming call numbers can be displayed on your TV, and you can pick up or ignore the call. How is that for call screening? (Sorry.)

This also will change in our offices soon, as more people work in hubs or grind through a project or presentation in a conference room or atrium of the building. SMART Boards (the whiteboards that download your scribbles into a printout or data file) will connect to your keyboard or tablet and become a video screen as well. Our work and data will come with us through cloud computing. Wi-Fi is less expensive and easier to install than local-area network wiring.

---

* Some of us are not meant to be seen in that level of detail. Remember Dustin Hoffman in the movie *Tootsie*? The producers were calling for a close-up "but not too close!"

Big, boxy desktop units and their nest of cables just add clutter and collect dust. We do not need them.

Friends recently told me how COWs will replace the computer labs in our schools. No longer will we need to dedicate fixed real estate in the school to a room with rows of computers and monitors; A computer on wheels (What did you think COW stood for?) is a cart with 20 laptops or tablet computers on it that can be shared among classrooms and is just wheeled from room to room per the schedule. Wi-Fi in the schools will allow all the computers to connect, and the kids are off to the races.[*]

PLASTIC BOTTLE USE WILL DECLINE 75% AND TAKE PAPER CUPS WITH IT BY 2018

We already know that we will be overrun by empty plastic water bottles before we retire if we do not start using them more responsibly soon. People are now filling up at home with reusable Nalgene or aluminum bottles. What about the plastic bottles from sport drinks and pop or soda? This is still a consumable, but I am not sure what the solution is. Pouches could work but still would involve some plastic. You could go to a refilling station and buy in bulk or packaging could evolve to the two- and four-liter bulk packs like we see with some wines, such as Gatorade in my cupboard with a little spigot that lets me dispense what I need today. Aluminum cans are very recyclable, as are glass bottles, but both take some energy to process back into the production version of the container again. I am not sure what is *Next* here, but somewhere, someone smart is working on it.

Worse than plastic to me are all the paper coffee cups we see in the garbage, on the sides of the streets. Dunkin' Donuts and Tim Horton's need to provide incentives to customers to use refillable mugs: knock a dime off the price of our coffee or pay a nickel to bring the paper cups back after use to have the store properly recycle them. Work with your suppliers to develop a cup that uses more postconsumer paper waste. Save some trees.

---

[*] Credit to Val Erskine, Kim Mahoney, and Teri Bonin.

Could we scan a consumer's license plate at the drive-through and print it on the cup? If it gets tossed on the side of the road, the "litter police" could trace it to you and levy a fine.[*]

"OCCUPY" MOVEMENT BECOMES A TAX REVOLT BY 2016

The Occupy movements in various cities caught global attention in 2011, but they were still driven by a small minority of the population. I expect that the situation will get worse, but with a clearer purpose over the next five years. This is not a call to arms—far from it. I think people are missing the point. To me, the problem is less about wage disparity and who gets taxed the most and more about what happens with those taxes when they are collected. The lack of transparency with government spending and the waste and complexity in the overall system (regardless of country) will come under increasing scrutiny as administrations are challenged for funding.

Some departments are doing very well and driving improvements to operations on an ongoing basis. A friend, for example, recently headed up Passport Canada while it drove a reduction in the time it takes for passport applications to be processed from six weeks to about two weeks. Think about the savings in time and labor here when the application touches fewer "desks" and spends less time sitting in a queue somewhere. Revenue Canada has done a nice job increasing efficiency in its operations as well. Why then, do I need to spend 90 minutes in line for my driver's license renewal, with the people on the desk processing about on average one application every 7 to 10 minutes? And, why are they in such a bad mood? While it takes two weeks for a new passport, my new driver's license arrived over four weeks later—waste. Provincial, state, and federal government branches *should* benchmark for best practices, cost, and time-saving processes.

We understand that the electoral cycle means that new administrations can be voted in every four years, which means some potential shift in policy and strategy and consequently some impact on operations. What we need to insist on, however, is that ongoing government

---

[*] Credit Don Warren.

operations run efficiently and we are treated as customers. I do not think that is too much to ask; it is our money they are spending, correct?

A REHUMANIZATION OF COMMUNICATION BY 2015*

Texting instead of talking; e-mailing someone in a cubicle 15 feet away; video chats—all are a result of great innovations in communication technology and appropriate for specific purposes, but society takes them too far. Communication is now far less personal and far less effective.

I have two perspectives on this; the first is that this is a result of antisocial tendencies buried deep within all of us, and the technology is just supporting that behavior. That is really for the sociologists to prove or disprove. Perhaps new forms of communication are just easier, and we are all lazy. Some will say it is more efficient. How do we get back to something more personal, however? Will it be a conscious effort by "innovators" in society? I do not have the answer.

TEN THINGS TO CREATE OR KILL

This section is for 10 ideas for innovation and, in the spirit of Lean, for discussion of some services and products to shut down to free up resources for new paths and opportunities.

Create: No-Brainer Food Labels We Can All Read

Understand when I say "no-brainer food labels we can all read," I mean read without our glasses. Maybe there could be a green circle somewhere obvious if it is healthy, a yellow circle if it will not kill you right away, and a red circle if we should only consume it while sitting next to a trained technician with a portable defibrillator.

While we are at it, someone needs to develop an app that allows us to program our dietary or health "plan"—bulking up, dropping 20 pounds, low-carb diet, diabetic diet, and so on—into our smart phone, and if we are unsure about a product on the store shelves or

---

* Courtesy of Steve Mercer.

at a friend's place for dinner, we can scan the bar code and get that green, yellow, or red circle.* Food contents or ingredients such as glutens, carbohydrates, and "bad" (LDL, or low-density lipoprotein) cholesterol need to become much more visible.

Kill: Cyberbullying

We could argue that our kids are spending too much time online anyway, but cyberbullying is a real problem. It is far too easy for negative comments to be posted and broadcast on social media like Facebook. At this point, it takes manual intervention to shut down the activity; someone has to report the events and circumstances and hope that the site shuts down those responsible. That takes time, and the instigators can just create a new account and get back on again.

We have "sniffer" software that screens for other types of inappropriate activity. Cyberbullying should get the same attention and technology to shut it down, including automatic and accepted reporting back to the offender's school, parents, or workplace.

Create: "Express" Departments in Grocery Stores

We all get that grocery store designers want us to walk through the entire store to get to the milk, bread, and eggs, things we run out of that drive us to do that "quick trip to the store." By walking through eight aisles to the back corner, we may see a few other things and pick them up on the way, thus increasing our purchase volume. On the other hand, by design, those stores are showing little respect for their customers' time. What if they created a small "express" section near the front corner of the store where you could whip in, pick up the essentials that you need right now, and get out in half the time—less lining up and arriving home sooner. Would that appeal to you? My premise with ideas like this is that we build customer enthusiasm when we make our customers' lives easier, not harder. Convenience stores like 7-Eleven prove this concept works, and the larger grocery stores are losing business to those chains. The store that does

---

* Given that there are roughly a million apps out there already for the iPhone, Android, and Blackberry, this one may already be there.

something like this will build satisfaction in the market, which will result in more trips to this store, rather than less, and when I do need to fill the grocery cart, I am going to that store.

Kill: The Facebook "Like-Me" Marketing

While I am on social media, and I will admit that this is not one of my strong points, the whole "Like" function seems a bit adolescent for companies to be using in their marketing initiatives. You have heard it on the radio: "Like us on Facebook!" I agree with a consumer having the ability to endorse a brand, with the firm eventually using it in advertising sales, as in, "See, we have 30,000 people who like us. That is why you need to advertise with this station." Clicking on the like function gives the customer access to promotions and contests. I get that, but asking for that endorsement just sounds needy to me.

Create: A Better Password System

How many passwords do you have? How often do you have to change them, or do you change them? We have them for online shopping, social media Web sites, e-mail accounts, systems at work, credit cards: wow! I do not know if it will be biometrics (fingerprint or retina scanners) or maybe a central security program on our computers where we log in once, and it logs into everything else we need, or something else. But, this seems to be getting more and more complicated, with passwords now being eight digits or longer, including numeric, symbols, and mixed upper- and lowercase letters. Mess it up a few times when you are logging in, and you are booted out of the system altogether. Someone help us please!

Create: Smarter, Synchronized Traffic Lights

Creating smarter, synchronized traffic lights is a big idea, but it seems to me that there should be a simpler solution out there somewhere for a lot of reasons. As a society, we are spending significant resources reducing our collective carbon footprint, yet one of the biggest contributors is the ever-increasing collective population of vehicles on the roads. More people means more cars means more traffic. Vehicle numbers are increasing everywhere faster than infrastructure can be built to support them: Remember the gridlock of transport trucks stuck on the freeways in China for almost two weeks in the summer of 2010? We cannot build roads fast enough to manage our vehicles.

Traffic circles and one-way streets have been around forever and solve some of these issues, but they can be impractical as a retrofit in many urban locations. Hybrid and electric cars will help this by having virtually zero emissions while idling in traffic. Governments are investigating high-speed rail systems that keep cars off the roads. These are all good, but not enough.

My question is, why am I still sitting at an intersection waiting at a red light when there are no vehicles crossing in front of me? This is so simple it is obscene. Put in cameras or weight sensors at all intersections and turn my light green if there is no one at the other corners. While we are at it, stop turning the light I am approaching red when no one is waiting to go the other way. Synchronize some of the lights on busy streets so that traffic moves rather than stopping at each light. Get the cars moving, and there is less traffic, less emissions.

GPS devices and our smart phones have improved this somewhat, helping us avoid busy or congested roads and intersections, but traffic light technology also needs to play a role. Different studies on waiting lines (including waiting in traffic) have us spending up to five years of our lives waiting in lines[1]; this has got to get some attention. Ultimately, this is a Lean problem to me—tons of waste in the system. Maybe we can get someone from Toyota to help us figure it out.

Kill: The "Reply All" Button

The "Reply All" button is a problem for all of us and something we fix together. Most organizations do not provide guidelines on the use or nonuse of Reply All, but perhaps they should. Think twice! Better yet, the gurus of e-mail software should force us to respond to an "Are you sure?" prompt any time we try the Reply All (or "Are you REALLY sure?" or "Force everyone to read what you have to say!"[*]).

Everyone in the firm does not need to hear that e-mail conversation.

---

[*] Courtesy Cheryl Green.

Create: Better Kitchen Timers

Maybe it is just in our house, but kitchen timers on your oven and microwave are obnoxious. They are unreasonably loud, beep at least five times, and are about as complicated to set as your old VCR (which is why most of our VCR clocks just flashed —). Yes, this one is a pet peeve.

Create: Doggie DNA Testing

Creating doggie DNA testing is courtesy of my brother-in-law Ross, and I love it. He is a dog owner and religiously "picks up" after his dog while walking the animal in public areas.* My parents, in-laws, and many of you do this as well, carrying plastic bags in your pockets and then lugging the dropping to the nearest trash can. Why then, are there so many unclaimed bombs on the sidewalks, paths, and parks? We know why: We see that dog owner walking a pet and then carrying on after Fido does his business without stooping and scooping. Bastard!

What Ross is looking for is a quick and inexpensive way to test the pets' DNA and then link the pet and its owner to the land mines on public property. Then, we can start returning that unclaimed property to its rightful owner. Admit it—you like this idea, and more than a few of you would volunteer to make the delivery. Picture the public employee walking through the parks, smiling at pet owners, bending down to pet the "nice doggie" while palming a small set of clippers to collect a bit of fur for the doggie DNA banks.

Create: Active Messaging on Clothing

The creation of active messaging on clothing is just for fun. While we are talking about the lack of dignity in picking up after a pet, what about peeling open the back of junior's diaper for a peek? There are lots of options here where the diaper's status is more easily visible.

---

* As an aside, one of the many reasons we do not own a dog is the fact we would have to pick up its droppings. Which species is in charge here, anyway? When aliens land (and they will) and observe us briefly before making that initial contact, they will assume the dogs are the supreme beings on the planet as the tall bipeds guard them and pick up their poop. What a way to start off an intergalactic relationship.

The diaper could change color when it is wet, and the colors could have meaning. The word *juicy* could become emblazoned on the infant's bum or *his* and *hers* to denote whether Dad or Mom, respectively, changes the diaper (packed randomly in the package; no more, "But I got the last one!"). There is moisture- and heat-sensitive technology that could be incorporated in these diapers. Proctor and Gamble is half-way there—in its Pampers Swaddlers, a strip turns green when the diaper is wet.

Better yet, take a page from the greeting card business and incorporate a song chip and cheap battery in the diaper. When the diaper fills, the bass riff from Queen's "Another One Bites the Dust" plays.

And, just so we do not wrap this section talking about diapers, the same technology could be used in clothing. Workout wear that changes color depending on the intensity of your workout, giving visible "credit" for more time and body heat on the treadmill. Maybe the words *fast* or *hot* appear or the athletic apparel company's name or logo, with a brand strategy something like, "You have to earn the right to wear our logo!" Coming soon?

NOTE

1. Fitzsimmons, J.A., and Fitzsimmons, M.J., *Service Management: Operations Strategy, Information Technology*, 6th edition, McGraw-Hill, New York, 2008.

Appendix 2: More Thoughts on Lean

This section is really intended to give you some more tools for the tool kit in the organization while you look to get more Lean and drive business process optimization. I preface this with the comment that I am a firm believer in getting a facilitator of some sort to kick it off. The leadership team and parts of the organization will have some natural resistance to pursuing this or put "roadblocks" in getting alignment toward your goals. First, they do not see the opportunities of the initiative as they are too close to the operations, perhaps too busy or involved in day-to-day operations; second, they can feel threatened by the process and how it may impact their areas of responsibility; and third, they envision a predetermined set of plans and needs or implied terms associated with how the group should proceed. These three characteristics represent paradigms and biases for the leadership team, and they are very common (in fact, I have never seen a leadership team, no matter how capable, that did not embody at least a couple of them). Basically, Lean is different enough from what they are used to that you typically need some outside support to initiate it.

Even the Japanese needed help with Lean when they first started down that path, and interestingly, they turned to an American, W. Edwards Deming, for that guidance. Deming, having been largely ignored by industry in the United States, was happy to help. After World War II, Japanese manufacturing facilities were decimated. Materials were scare, millions of people were out of work, and products were viewed as of poor quality. Between 1950 and 1970, Deming and his followers turned that around in Japan with a rigorous focus on quality: identify and fix the problem, eliminate waste, and continuously improve, with the "Deming cycle" (Plan, Do, Check, Act) becoming the hallmark of Lean for the rest of the world. The Japanese had no excess available at all, so they figured out how to be the best with what they had. How do we do that here?

Starting with a facilitator, speaker, or trainer is the first step in getting people to open their eyes to the opportunities in front of the organization. Make that part of an off-site meeting or retreat with the executive team. Begin with a connection between the vision of the organization—strategy, where are we going, key issues—and how Lean will support the process. That group needs to understand that Lean is part of how we succeed with innovation, execution, projects, and day-to-day operations; it is the enabler for those key functions, freeing up the resources we need to be successful. Figure A2.1 highlights that relationship.

The ultimate direction your organization takes with Lean and getting it kicked off depends on you and your organizational culture. We talked about a number of tactics in Chapter 2 to start to shift some of those paradigms among the team: the awareness test video, the Lean alphabet, and 5S. The next steps are up to you.

The following are suggestions of where to look for help:

- Jeff Liker has written a great series of books, *The Toyota Way* series (McGraw-Hill, New York, 2003), including the original classic *Toyota Talent* (2007) and *The Toyota Way Fieldbook* (2005) (these two with coauthor David Meier). Liker did an excellent job translating some of the mystique behind Toyota's approach to eliminating waste, which is the heart

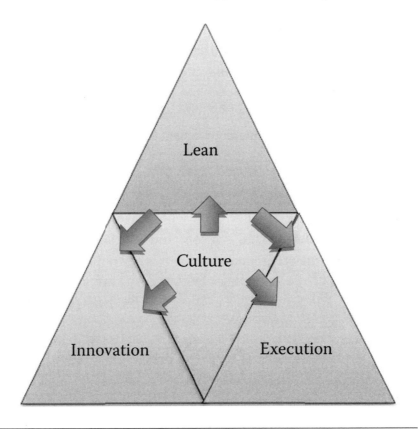

Figure A2.1 Lean and the Enabled Organization.

of the Toyota Production System. The examples in the books are manufacturing and product related, but they really apply to all of our organizations. While you are benchmarking outside your industry, start with reading *The Toyota Way*.

- Any research and consideration of Lean should include the names James Womack and Daniel Jones, who gained recognition with their work, *The Machine That Changed the World* (Macmillan/Rawson, New York, 1990). Check out their later works directly on Lean, including *Lean Thinking* (2003) and *Lean Solutions* (2005) (both Simon and Schuster).

- While he was at it, Womack created the Lean Enterprise Institute (LEI) (http://www.lean.org), a not-for-profit organization geared to spreading Lean education and ideas to all industries. LEI offers training in the form of clinics and seminars on specific Lean tactics and fundamentals and will run custom programs at your facility.

- There are literally hundreds of organizations now offering Lean and Lean Six Sigma training, both in person and online. Keep in mind that to do this properly, it takes commitment, which means an online course or a half-day session somewhere will not get the job done for you. This is an ongoing process that, like innovation or execution, requires a culture shift across the whole organization. So, talk to peers and colleagues: who did they work with, what did they like or dislike, and so on. Find someone you are comfortable with before signing on to a long-term development plan.
- Attend conferences on the subject; they are everywhere now and often industry specific (there is a big Lean Six Sigma conference on health care every year in New Orleans, for example). Connect with industry professionals through associations like the Production and Operations Management Society (http://www.poms.org).
- Journals such as *Harvard Business Review, MIT Sloan Management Review,* and *Ivey Business Journal* regularly have pieces focused on driving Lean in different ways through the organization.

As you start this process within your organization, you will hear the comment very frequently that the concepts and materials employed in Lean are very simple, and they are. Simple, however, is not easy, so organizational leadership needs to make sure that they are committed and doing it for the right reasons. Talk to people who understand Lean and help them understand your business. What are the issues, and where are the opportunities? Make sure this is right for you and then develop a plan to break those paradigms and drive it through the organization. In support of your vision, the plan needs to include the Message, the Methods, and the Mandate.

The Message, again, is why we are doing it. Perhaps it is the market, the competitive realities, the scarcity of available talent, or even better, to support our efforts in innovation. Maybe it is about survival. Keep the message simple and go back to it again and again.

The Methods are the tactics you employ to drive Lean. These could and should involve both leadership training and employee training. A Lean Champion is identified at the senior levels of the organizations. Objectives are matched to goals, which are visible on the Balanced Score Card. People see Lean, they talk about it, and the firm celebrates the victories. Resources freed up are quickly mobilized where they can make an impact somewhere else.

The Mandate is the consistency with which you drive the initiative. Expect the shift in culture and behavior, and the attainment of the desired results, to take a couple of years, and even then you will not be done. As clichéd as it sounds, this is a journey. With that in mind, are you prepared to start it?

As you get into Lean, one common element that practitioners will talk about is the value chain (or value stream), which is basically just what it sounds like. Picture any process in your operations, from assembling a computer to paying a supplier invoice. Say that process has eight steps in it. Draw out the steps in the process on a whiteboard or piece of paper. Measure the time it takes to complete all those steps (a great tool here is to video record the team completing the work).

How much of the time in that process is actually productive? That is, how much time in the process is actually spent creating value: adding components, testing the computer, loading the software, and so on. Those tasks add value. Maybe the total productive time in that process is 10 minutes. So, why does it take us 40 minutes to assemble the computer? The waste in the system comes from the non-value-added activities: waiting for parts to arrive at a workstation, repairing a nonspec part, even the five seconds spent walking up the line to pick up a part for an assembly. All of that time is wasted according to Lean and does not add value.

The true test of value, when the team is talking about the process, is whether the customer would pay for that step. Should the customer pay for rework? Does the customer want to pay for idle time, wasted motion, or moving inventory six times before it gets shipped? Of course not. This is your waste and the key area of focus as you start to drive Lean.

Most of us have processes or departments we know to be Lean Opportunities around the firm. Avoid the temptation, however, to just jump into "fixing" that process until you have properly framed the activity. Again, use the Message, Methods, and Mandate. Start with the awareness test or something similar and let people get used to the idea before threatening their pet processes. Ask for their input and put people from each process on the Lean team. Initiatives with engaged, involved employees will be far more successful with deeper and longer-lasting results.

As we did with innovation, there are some "calisthenics" we can start with in our own behavior that help us work in more of a Lean fashion. Think about these ideas in your own day-to-day activities (and let me know if you have others).

PERSONAL LEAN TACTICS

There are some Lean tactics we can use personally. Never buy more hangers when you get new clothes; if you have not worn something in two years, donate it or throw it away. Recycle the extra hangers in your closets now, before they become occupied.

If something is moved more often than it is used, do you really need it? The same goes for things you have to walk around more than use.

Get rid of your old audio cassettes and VHS movies. You will never listen to them again, and while *Beverly Hills Cop* is a classic, it will never be a collectible.

Have you noticed how so many self-storage facilities are popping up around your city or neighborhood? This is huge business, but it is dependent on the amount of "stuff" we all hang on to for its survival (hit YouTube for a look at George Carlin and his gag on "stuff"; you have probably seen it before, but it cuts to the center of this and is very funny). If you are moving or renovating, you may need storage. Perhaps you have some seasonal gear that does not fit in your apartment or condo, but you do use it. Both are reasonable uses for third-party storage. If you have stored it for two years and have not needed it, however, sell it or give it away and save your money.

We all have money, time, behavior, and procedures tied up in the complexities of our lives. This is a fundamental opportunity. Whether it is about your organization or personal lives, allow yourself and the people around you to focus on fewer things, but expect better performance. Give them time to be creative, yet ask for something exceptional.

Simple is good.

Index